Reflections on Crisis: The Role of the Public Intellectual

D1423662

REFLECTIONS ON CRISIS:
The Role of the Public Intellectual

edited by
Mary P. Corcoran
and Kevin Lalor

Reflections on Crisis: The Role of the Public Intellectual

First published 2012

by Royal Irish Academy
19 Dawson Street
Dublin 2

www.ria.ie

ISBN 978-1-908996-06-0

Printed in Ireland by Turner Print Group.

CONTENTS

ACKNOWLEDGEMENTS

The Academy Committee for Social Sciences wishes to thank the Royal Irish Academy for supporting and facilitating the 2009 half-day symposium: 'Public Intellectuals in Times of Crisis: What Do They Have to Offer?', which led to this publication. Quotations reproduced in this book were excerpted from a transcript of the discussion. The Committee is particularly grateful to the National University of Ireland Publications Committee for providing a grant for this publication. The Committee would like to thank Professor Mary P. Corcoran, Professor Vani Borooah, Dr Kevin Lalor and Mr Justice Adrian Hardiman for their efforts in organising the symposium and in bringing the publication to fruition. The Committee also wishes to thank the speakers at the symposium and the subsequent contributors to this volume, including Professor Tom Garvin, Mr Donncha O'Connell, Professor Pat O'Connor, Professor Liam O'Dowd and Professor Frances Ruane. The Committee is indebted to the staff of the Royal Irish Academy, especially Dr John Maguire, Programme Manager of the Committee, and Ms Ruth Hegarty, Ms Helena King and Ms Rosie Duffy.

The views expressed here are those of the authors and do not necessarily reflect those of the Academy Committee for Social Sciences, or the Royal Irish Academy.

THE ACADEMY COMMITTEE FOR SOCIAL SCIENCES 2008–12

The Academy Committee for Social Sciences is one of seventeen multidisciplinary committees of the Royal Irish Academy concerned with the organisation and development of their respective disciplines and with providing an interface between Ireland and the relevant international bodies. It has a remit to pursue strategic and policy development within the social sciences on an all-Ireland basis. The Committee has been involved in organising a number of conferences and symposia, including a lecture by Professor Charles Bosk on 'Problems, Puzzles and Paradoxes in Research Ethics' (2009) and the publication of a number of policy reports including the report on 'Evaluating Research Performance in Economics and Social Sciences' (2007).

Members

Professor Vani Kant Borooah, MRIA (Chair)
Professor Mary P. Corcoran
Professor David Dickson, MRIA
Professor Tom Garvin, MRIA
Dr David Getty
The Hon. Mr Justice Adrian Hardiman, MRIA
Dr Karen Keaveney
Dr Kevin Lalor (Secretary)
Dr Pete Lunn
Dr Fiona Magowan
Professor Siniša Malešević, MRIA
Dr Orlaigh Quinn
Dr Theresa Reidy
Dr Kevin Sweeney
Professor Brendan J. Whelan

Programme Manager

Dr John Maguire

Conference Organising Committee

Professor Vani Borooah
Dr Kevin Lalor
Professor Mary P. Corcoran

'I can't remember who said it to me but the difference between this crisis and the ones in the 1950s and 1980s is that this time it is everywhere else as well. Back in the 1950s we were on our own. We were brilliantly original in having a disaster while everyone else was having a boom. This time we are sharing our glory with everyone else but we are just being a bit better at it than the others. There is nowhere to run this time, there is nowhere to emigrate to. The Americans are in a fix too.'

TOM GARVIN

'We need to be self-critical. Could we have done better? How could we have done better? We pushed the debate along, but we failed ultimately for a number of reasons. We had the wrong strategy, or perhaps even no strategy as public intellectuals. We had polite but not terribly politic tactics. We had poor logistics and poor support as public intellectuals. We did not go out of our way to build a wider consensus.'

BRIAN LUCEY

'What has led to the decline of public intellectuals is the same thing that has lead to the decline of pubs. We used to have a lot more 'third spaces' where people could move beyond class, beyond gender, beyond their workaday norm, and maybe look at their private lives too from another space entirely. But that type of encounter is happening less and less.'

DECLAN KIBERD

INTRODUCTION:
CHALLENGING INTELLECTUALS

Mary P. Corcoran

Department of Sociology, National University of Ireland, Maynooth

> Intellectuals are challenged, I believe now to a moral choice, to drift into, be part of, a consensus that accepts a failed paradigm of life and economy or to offer, or seek to recover, the possibility of alternative futures (President Michael D. Higgins, speech to the National University of Ireland, 25 January 2012).

In his book *Ill fares the land*, Tony Judt muses on the erosion of values-based politics and the concomitant ascent of market fundamentalism in western societies. He asks whether politics can be re-fashioned in order to re-create a social contract fit for purpose in the twenty-first century. This question is particularly pertinent in the Irish context as we reflect ruefully on the fate of the country over the last five years. The orthodoxies associated with the Celtic Tiger have come unstuck and austerity has replaced our chimerical prosperity. The current crisis has created a space for review and reflection on how we got to where we are, and where we might go from here. The opening of a space for such self-critical reflection is crucial to any process of transformation. What are the lessons to be gleaned from our recent history? Do we have the imagination to reconfigure our economy and society in such a way that the interests of the public at large take precedence over those of a select few private individuals? Whom might we look to for guidance, vision and the tools of analysis to embark on a re-imagining process? This short volume seeks to contribute to this task by exploring the role that public intellectuals may play in public life, particularly during times of crisis.

This volume is the outcome of a symposium held at the Royal Irish Academy in November 2009, the purpose of which was to explore—in a public forum and in a multidisciplinary context—public intellectualism (or the lack of it) in Irish life. Speakers from a range of disciplinary and institutional perspectives presented thoughtful and cogent accounts of the relationship between the academy, the market and the public sphere in an era marked by what literary scholar Declan Kiberd described as 'a privatisation of all experiences and the impoverishment of intellectual life.' A lively debate ensued. It was clear that the event touched a chord with those present. In bringing together five of the key presentations alongside some of the insights contributed by other invited speakers on the day, we hope to provide a catalyst for further reflection, rumination and debate. Too often events of this nature disappear into the ether once the meeting room has emptied and we have all departed for home. In documenting and disseminating some of the insights offered at the symposium 'Public Intellectuals at a Time of Crisis', we hope to contribute to the important debates which enliven the public sphere.

Public intellectuals are in a unique position to build a bridge between the world of academia and the general public, to communicate ideas and analyses that can illuminate and help people to deepen their understanding of the world around them. As the great American sociologist C. Wright Mills argued, neither the life of the individual nor the history of a society can be understood, without understanding both. Public intellectuals help us to understand the connections between our individual biographical narratives and the historical, social and economic forces that help to shape them.

This is all the more germane during a time of crisis when people are facing new challenges such as job loss, reduction in income, uncertainty and insecurity about the future. It is at times like these that people want some explanation for what has happened and some indications of where we might be going as a society and an economy. It is particularly during uncertain times such as the present that we need to promote informed debate within the wider public sphere. Public intellectuals potentially play a significant role in this process by putting forward moral frameworks and schemes of interpretation which are accessible to the wider public. Their clear-sighted insights offered without fear or favour can guide us as we attempt to come to terms with the present and begin reshaping our collective future.

The contributors to this volume represent all that is best about Irish academia and are drawn from universities across the whole island of Ireland. Each addresses a set of pertinent questions: in an era where the notion of 'the public' has been seriously undermined, is there still a role for the public intellectual? If so, what form should that role take in the twenty-first century? How can public intellectuals adapt their message to audiences increasingly fragmented by the technological and media transformations in society? What innovations are required to disseminate knowledge to wider publics?

What role can public intellectuals play in fomenting informed debate in society?

The collection holds a mirror to the current economic crisis and serves up some chilling home truths. The contributors examine the economic, social, and, indeed, moral dilemmas facing Ireland. More specifically, they explore the vexed question of what academic intellectuals have to contribute to the resolution of crisis and the constraints under which they operate. The insights to be gleaned from these contributions provide food for thought on the role of public intellectuals not just here in Ireland, but in modern democracies more generally. They provide a framework of interpretation that allows us to consider the impact of similar crises in other jurisdictions. They remind us elegantly and forcefully that ideas matter.

Writing from the purview of an academic lawyer, Donncha O'Connell explores the implications of 'creeping managerialism' within the Irish academy. He carefully dissects the role of academics as public intellectuals and the value to society of critical thinking. He offers an overview of the changes that have occurred in universities in recent years, demonstrating how those changes have helped to reshape the traditional mission of the university, a theme also taken up by Tom Garvin in his contribution. Both attest to a scenario in which universities increasingly privilege technocratic knowledge production, at the expense of the humanities and the social sciences. According to O'Connell the dearth of university-bred intellectuals in Irish public life is at least in part attributable to the obsessive focus on key performance indicators which measure 'academic output' in an intellectually restrictive way. Challenging 'Orwellian' thinking within the university, O'Connell argues for a set of more open and pluralist requirements for what it is to be a good academic. He argues that think-tanks create a space in which public intellectualism can flourish because they are adept at translating intellectual capital into political strategies and public policy initiatives.

In a provocative contribution amplifying some of the themes introduced by O'Connell, Tom Garvin asserts that intellectuals are only valued when things have become unstuck. In the good times, they tend to be ignored. The first role of the public intellectual is to encourage or even force people to think, but according to Garvin there has always been a strain of anti-intellectualism in Irish life. In his view, the value of education, as distinct from practical training for earning one's living, has never been fully grasped in independent Ireland. Garvin decries a trend that he sees underway (and not exclusively in Ireland) whereby many universities are coming under increased pressure to engage in applied, intellectually derivative and profitable research at the expense of free enquiry. He sees this as tantamount to the destruction of imagination and a veritable assault on university intellectual life.

Mindful of Richard Posner's framework for understanding the different ways in which public intellectuals may be drawn into public discourse, Frances Ruane reflects on the manner in which Irish academic economists performed in public debate and in the media during the onset of the economic crisis. She notes the uneasy relationship which often prevails between academics and journalists who operate to very different timelines. Economists rose to the challenges presented by the crisis, she argues, contributing opinion pieces to the traditional media, participating in public seminars and going 'head to head' with their peers in the blogosphere. The crisis,

Ruane concludes, served to reconnect the economics profession more directly with the economy, as it has done
with the entire academic community.

Drawing on Sartre's aphorism that if an intellectual is
to understand his society he must adopt the point of view
of its most underprivileged members, Pat O'Connor
argues that public intellectuals at least in theory should be
concerned with creating new agendas and raising issues
that those in power seek to avoid. Moreover, she suggests
that public intellectuals have a key role to play in transforming what C. Wright Mills called 'private troubles' into
'public issues.' O'Connor raises concerns about the crisis
of legitimacy within the state, and what she sees as the key
fault lines of gender and class. She questions the normal-
isation of a patriarchal political system, and documents
the myriad ways in which gender inequality is reproduced—often unquestioningly—within Irish society and
the university system. She opines that since the institutional elite of Irish society has remained relatively stable
across time (despite economic, social and cultural change)
there is little likelihood of it producing from within its
ranks critical public intellectuals who might question the
basis of elitism. Echoing Ruane and O'Connell,
O'Connor notes that there is a tension between the
increasingly specialist nature of knowledge required in
universities, and the wider activities that public intellectuals might undertake, whether in critical reflection or
public dialogue. The introduction of metrics to measure
academic productivity provides a further disincentive to
build connections with wider society and engage in social
action. And even if academics and public intellectuals are
motivated to engage, there is, according to O'Connor, an
absence of a public arena in which to do so. She calls on

public intellectuals to promote the notion of fairness as a cornerstone of society. She asks that public intellectuals address themselves to issues of gender and class, and that they strive to mobilise greater community awareness through a more robust media presence.

The concept of accountability is central to Liam O'Dowd's contribution. He notes that with the global and local crises of financial capital, the contradictions associated with abdicating accountability to the capitalist markets are becoming ever more apparent. While acknowledging the important role public intellectuals may play in exposing corruption and malfeasance, O'Dowd forensically traces structural and historical factors that serve to limit the influence of public intellectuals and diminish the possibility of their mounting a sustained critique of the existing political and economic system. In the Irish context, he notes the formative influences of the Irish national movement, British imperialism and the Catholic Church on public intellectuals. O'Dowd delineates four key crises in the history of the state that have been critical to the formation of Irish intellectuals and the debates that have preoccupied them: the economic collapse of the 1950s, the eruption of the Troubles in Northern Ireland in the 1970s, the economic recession of the 1980s and the current global capitalist crisis. O'Dowd concludes that the progressive economisation of public debates, the general enthrallment to consumer capitalism and its co-optation of the state, politics and culture have combined to marginalise the role of public intellectuals in accountability and democracy.

All of the contributors observe that the role of the public intellectual has come under pressure due to the advancement of technocratic and instrumental knowledge and through the popularisation of tropes such as 'knowledge society' and 'smart economy'. Moreover, the marketisation of society has posed a major challenge to public intellectuals who have found it increasingly difficult (or in some cases inconvenient) to inhabit the role of social critic. As Declan Kiberd observes, the public sphere has been abandoned by all kinds of people and humanists have failed to adequately defend the humanities.

Sociologist and public intellectual Michael Burawoy has argued that the pressures of instrumentalisation threaten the tradition of the public university and by extension the role of the public intellectual. He argues passionately that reflexivity should be asserted as a counterweight to instrumentality by bringing the various forms of academic knowledge production—substantive professional knowledge, advocacy policy knowledge, traditional public knowledge and disciplinary critical knowledge—into more systematic, mutually reinforcing relationships with each other. Such a move would enhance the university's role as a mediator of deliberative democracy and would strengthen the critical public sphere.

There is a recognition amongst our contributors that the term 'public intellectual' is an inherently problematic one. There is an absence of consensus on what precisely a public intellectual is, and to what degree one can exert influence. This is partly to do with changing contexts. The North American sociologist Neil McLaughlin suggests that the 'structures of appreciation' have altered across history and that there is less space available now for public intellectuals. Nevertheless, individually and collectively our contributors point to the possibilities open to public intellectuals to play a proactive role in pushing for fairness in society, democratic reform and greater accountability.

Declan Kiberd avers that accounts of our recent economic collapse contain the master narrative of a solution: greater regulation accompanied by a values shift that would move us beyond individualism and towards a more ethically-based, wider vision of society. That re-visioning project constitutes a central element of Michael D. Higgins's presidency. Indeed, in a speech to the National University of Ireland on the occasion of his conferral with an Honorary Doctorate, President Higgins asserted that the

> paradigm drawn from the fiction of rational markets needs to be replaced by a scholarship that is genuinely emancipatory, centred on originality rather than imitation, one that, for example, restores the unity between the sciences and culture in their common human curiosity, discovery and celebration of the life of the mind' (Higgins, 2012).

These concerns are both implicit and explicit in the contributions to this volume. Several of the contributors allude to the excessive focus on 'managerialism' in contemporary public discourse at the expense of a more humanistic, social justice perspective. Moreover, they question the preoccupation with *homo economicus* and the concomitant neglect of an understanding of the individual as a social, political, moral and cultural actor. Taken together, their insights suggest that we are richer for having public intellectuals in our midst. At a time of crisis in particular, we rely on the critique and creativity that public intellectuals can proffer. Finally, if we are to prosper as a people in the coming decades it is imaginative thinking that must be at the core of the renewal project.

'To me an intellectual is somebody who uses both a knowledge base—
and it is crucial that there should be some disciplinary knowledge base
whatever that may be—but also emotions, personal experiences,
politics. Those are, from an intellectual perspective, perfectly valid
inputs into the argument, into the intellectual discourse that
one wishes to engage in.'

BRIAN LUCEY

'I can think of examples of public intellectuals within my own experience playing very important roles, both positive and negative ones.
I can think of the contribution made by university lecturers and more
importantly university students in the institution I worked in
Johannsburg in the development of the trade union movement in the
late 1970s and early 1980s…South African academics also made
an important contribution to the spreading of democratic
norms among white South Africans.'

TOM LODGE

'An intellectual is someone who ought to be able to take a step
outside of inherited social class, outside of gender, outside of
national and religious traditions themselves, in order to
interrogate all of these things.'

DECLAN KIBERD

WITHIN AND BEYOND THESE WALLS: UNIVERSITY ACADEMICS AS PUBLIC INTELLECTUALS

Donncha O'Connell*

School of Law, National University of Ireland, Galway

INTRODUCTION

W hen I was invited to contribute to this volume my instant reaction was to disclaim any attachment to the idea of being a public intellectual. All of my initial notes on the subject construed the idea of a public intellectual in pejorative terms which, in itself, was a 'finding' of sorts. I thought of academics who happened to be public intellectuals in the following terms: escapees; trespassers; promiscuous talkers or 'pundits' (i.e. paid promiscuous talkers); exiles from the specific seeking refuge in the general; and credible 'notice-boxes' (this is a concept known only to those of us taught by nuns!).

The therapist inside my head—always alert to the dangers of self-loathing brought on by idle speculation—prompted me to do some research on the subject on which there is a substantial literature, much of it American and sociological. There you will find the idea of the public intellectual discussed in terms of specialists speaking beyond their usual 'audience' and often beyond their fields

* This paper was written when the author was a Visiting Senior Fellow at the Centre for the Study of Human Rights, London School of Economics and Political Science (LSE) in 2009–10.

of specialism. This is especially noteworthy when done by scientists who talk about the ethical as opposed to the informational aspects of science, apparently. One commentator, Alan Lightman, writes in hierarchical terms about three levels of public intellectual—plainly named Levels 1, 2 and 3—with people like Noam Chomsky and Edward Said in the Level 3 category. It is, for those who are interested, possible to progress 'slowly and even unconsciously' upwards from one level to the next in order to die happily as a Level 3 public intellectual. Others (like Joffe, 2003) speak of public intellectuals as 'general practitioners of the mind'. Presumably, like other GPs, they self-medicate with books and, if they happen to be academics, treat students as surrogate patients. Richard Posner (2001), a very prolific lawyer, characterises academic public intellectuals as 'peripheral insiders' or 'insiders pretending to be outsiders' and, on the basis of his own empirical analysis, is generally negative about their contribution in the United States.

Of course, it would be wrong to proceed on the assumption that public intellectuals are necessarily or even often academics. In fact, it can be argued, for reasons to which I will return, that contemporary Irish universities are unlikely places in which to find public intellectuals. The world of journalism, inhabited as it is by columnists and freelance pundits of varied intellectual prowess, has an undeniable tradition of public intellectualism. People like Karl Marx, Mark Twain and George Orwell were undoubtedly public intellectuals but they were undoubtedly journalists too. A similar tradition has been maintained in Irish journalism by figures like Seán Ó Faoláin, Desmond Fennell and Fintan O'Toole. It should, perhaps, be no surprise that media professionals are often better at mediated engagement with the public than those working in the comparatively rarefied atmosphere of academic institutions.

ARE UNIVERSITIES COLD HOUSES
FOR PUBLIC INTELLECTUALS?

The focus of this paper is on the role of academics as public intellectuals. As professionals, people live in, and are defined by, their professional context. Thus, if there is a reason why so few academics are public intellectuals it may have something to do with the university environments in which they work. Separation of the academic dancer from the university dance has not yet been successfully accomplished by any experimental alchemist but (drawing on universal truths, as revealed so accurately in David Lodge's novels) it is possible to ruminate productively. Academics exist professionally in universities, and work within academic units, usually within one unit of primary affiliation like a Faculty, Department, School or Centre. Thus, after announcing that one is an academic, the reflexive, almost existentialist, response is: 'What Department are you in?' Immediately, one is defined by one's departmental specialism, reflecting the organising principle of universities once memorably described as a series of independent sovereignties linked by a heating system. (In the case of my own university it is not a very good heating system but that is of no metaphorical significance!).

Universities have for some time embraced what Kronman (2007) calls a 'research ideal', founded upon disciplinary specialisation having moved from a culture of 'secular humanism', which itself had replaced an 'age of piety' and the scholastic tradition. It is arguable that the embrace of the so-called research ideal has entailed an abandonment of scholarship or, at least, a diminution in status of individual scholarship that is not quantifiable as research. How many times have you read university policy documents with phrases like: 'The University is committed to interdisciplinary, collaborative research on an inter-institutional basis while *respecting* individual scholarly endeavour…going forward'. For 'respect' read 'tolerate' and note the unsubtle construction of a new norm understandable by reference to the eccentricity that it replaces… going forward!

It could, of course, be argued that this 'new' research ideal involving collaboration across disciplines and between institutions is exactly what is needed to turn academics into higher functioning public intellectuals ranging freely across disciplines without frontiers, although no one would be so naive as to say this. To make such an assertion would miss the point of such research, as orchestrated through competitive funding bids, and would also miss the point of what it takes to make a public intellectual.

In Ireland, third-level research funding initiatives have been preoccupied with establishing and building a research infrastructure and contributing to 'the knowledge economy' or 'the smart economy'. There is nothing intrinsically wrong with this. In fact, it makes good business sense to blue-skies philanthropists and, perhaps, to hesitant state funders. However, there is an undoubted bias in favour of natural sciences and engineering of various kinds in such *core* funding drives that confirms and embeds a pre-existing weakening of the humanities, broadly understood, in the third-level sector. The implications of this for the intellectual life of a university are obvious.

Irish universities and ITs have bought into an emphasis on added-value research—with all of the connotations of 'excellence', in the Orwellian sense, that this entails—

leaving them open to the risk of becoming the R&D wing
of the state. This is not as monopolistic as it sounds when
one considers the emphasis on partnerships with industry,
but that hardly lessens the cause for concern in terms of
independence and the sharing of public benefits of such
applied research.

Education, at all levels, must be more than an instru-
ment of state industrial policy. Universities have a moral
purpose beyond the imperatives of flexibility and institutional survival. For those of us who work as academics
in universities, it is vital to re-establish an open and pluralist appreciation of what it is to be a good academic. By
that, I do not mean that what passes for good teaching
should be patronised with awards, or that the happen-
stance of wider community benefits that leak out of
universities should be branded or sold as commodifiable
'civic engagement'. It should still be possible to be a good
academic—and, therefore, a successful one—by inspir-
ing others to learn through scholarship grounded in a
genuine passion for one's subject, whether broad or
narrow. That should be the 'key performance indicator'
and not whether, in a survey of opinions, nine out of ten
student 'customers' who expressed a preference said your
course met their expectations or that they liked you. It
is harder to measure, in numerical terms, the success or
failure of an academic according to this more open and
pluralist set of requirements, but it is an infinitely more
meaningful standard and, surprisingly, harder to manip-
ulate than what passes for teaching evaluation now.

It should not be maverick or odd to say this although
it can, at times, sound like special pleading. My argument
is not one against change—a fairly predictable accusa-
tion—but one in favour of preserving the positive

elements of the current system, which could be jeopardised by the wrong kind of change.

The experience of Law Schools in Irish university restructuring drives is instructive. In all NUI universities former Law Faculties were coupled with former Faculties of Commerce without any convincing explanation, beyond the fact that it had been done elsewhere. Some blame UCD as it was the first to force such a marriage of administrative convenience. The informing mantra of university restructuring was that a smaller number of larger units would be more efficient (for which read: 'manageable'), making universities more 'fit for purpose', that 'purpose' remaining somewhat ill-defined although knowable through some clever decoding of strategic plans. This was, of course, a highly debateable engineering proposition that was only ever really debated in local political terms.

Any individual who served a period as dean during university restructuring, and thus bears a commensurate level of emotional scars (visible only to other deans!), probably sympathises and agrees with the desire to make academic units more manageable and more connected to an agreed university mission. However, there are some who remain unconvinced that this can be achieved by melding barely cognate units. The other reason put forward in favour of mergers was that levels of interdisciplinary academic activity would increase. This seems both fanciful and disingenuous, especially in the cases of law and commerce.

Law is an ancient discipline that draws on and is open to other disciplines. It can be intellectually rich and is, undoubtedly, a source of monetary riches to universities and other institutions offering law programmes. It also attracts students who are often as animated by the desire to be rich as the desire to do justice. (In this it differs little from vocations like medicine or dentistry where the opportunities for doing justice are obviously weaker!). In a world where knowledge is (allegedly) power, legal knowledge can also be a ticket to power—the ideal of 'a government of laws and not of men' permitting distinct advantages or privileges to 'legal men'—a most apposite observation in the case of the US.

In fairness to legal academics, they are no strangers to the public square, but it does not follow that they are more likely than other academics to be public intellectuals, despite the utility of their discipline and its broad relevance to public affairs. The usual role for a legal academic commentator, whether in the written or broadcast media, is to explain or comment upon the outcome of a case or some legislative proposal. In the US this can earn one minor celebrity status depending on how 'colourful' the media performances are and how controversial one is prepared to be (by, for example, articulating the appropriate measure of legal torture allowable to extract confessions from terrorists).

In Ireland, constitutional referendums are especially good for business, with lawyers—both academic and professional—adopting positions of inevitable prominence and sometimes even forming groups with titles (that would surely constitute nightmares for advertising experts) like 'Lawyers for this' or 'Lawyers against that'. That is to say nothing of the deservedly controversial role performed by judges acting as Referendum Commissions of one or more, a topic for another discussion, hopefully.

The banking crisis that is now an economic crisis has been a field day for economist commentators of various kinds but lawyers have been relatively less visible and vocal despite the centrality of legal issues as causal factors in the banking crisis and the undoubted relevance of law to what is proffered by way of partial solution in the form of NAMA. Whether or not the very public intervention by a group of academic economists in opposition to the NAMA proposals was well made, it was disappointing to see their views rudely dismissed at the time as merely 'academic', especially by an academic then working directly as an adviser to the minister for finance. This was no better than the intemperate and dismissive approach adopted some years previously by the former taoiseach Bertie Ahern to the warnings of some economists and business journalists that the apparent economic boom was perhaps more fragile and illusory than it seemed at the time.

Equally, it would appear that some economists show insufficient appreciation of the complexities of politics and the uniquely difficult job of being a politician. The same might be said of all public intellectuals operating at a safe remove from politics. Legal academics are adept at criticising judgments and legislative proposals without having ever been involved in a real case or experiencing the practical difficulties of legislative drafting. This may partially explain the reactive anti-intellectualism evident in Irish politics, though it does not validate it.

A PRAGMATIC 'WAY FORWARD'

Much of this paper, thus far, has been observational and critical, leaving the author open to the charge of being 'another useless academic' hurling on the rhetorical ditch. If making public intellectuals more relevant means making ideas more important, then there is a greater role to be performed by public intellectuals who happen to be academics, and not just in times of crisis. There is plenty of public engagement by specialist academics in their chosen areas and, depending on the area of special-ism and the manner in which the 'message' is mediated, this can sometimes constitute engagement of a public intellectual kind. More often than not, engagement is reactive (for example to some 'crisis'), by which time the more 'prophetic' nature of some academic or scholarly writing or research, yet to be publicly amplified, is belat-edly acknowledged (such as the controversy that erupted a number of years ago and endures since, in relation to strict liability sexual offences involving minors). This has its place and may be regarded by some as *the* appropriate public role for academics but it should not rule out a more active engagement by academics in public affairs, whether controversial or not.

If we accept that universities, organised around narrow specialisms (even if now existing in larger administrative units) and driven by a funded research ideal are, in certain senses, constitutive of the behaviour of those working within them, then certain consequences follow. It is more likely that one will realise one's professional ambitions by being a specialist in a favoured area doing value-added research in response to funding tenders or some kind of 'out-sourced' research function of a state body that is respected and income-generating. No matter how 'excel-lent' one is, this does not leave much time for being a public intellectual. In certain situations, being a public intellectual may damage your standing as a potential earner of income for your employer by reason of a real or attributed under-mining of rigour and independence. But that does *not* mean that academics with something to offer cannot find some space for making a contribution of a public intellectual kind beyond the strictures of such 'core' research activities most favoured by academic institutions. Locating that space may be a problem and some pragmatism may be in order as it is unlikely that there will be a radical reversal of the culture shift just described in Irish universities.

If we look to periods where ideas mattered a lot, and these were not necessarily good periods or good ideas, we find that 'think-tanks' of various kinds were pivotal. Although there are some think-tanks in Ireland (for example Think Tank for Action on Social Change (Ireland) (TASC) and the Iona Institute) it could hardly be said that there is anything approximating to a think-tank culture in Irish politics or even in public policy discourse. Academics who might contribute to the work of such think-tanks, whether on a full-time or associate basis, and, thereby, make a contribution of a public intellectual kind, would search in vain for such opportunities in Ireland. As for popular awareness, one would be hard-pressed to find members of the Irish public who could name one Irish think-tank apart from, perhaps, the Economic and Social Research Institute (ESRI).

In the United Kingdom, the Thatcher period was demonstrably influenced by the work of the Centre for Policy Studies and its guru, Keith Joseph, among others. Now we perhaps await a conservative resurrection personified by the nice Mr Cameron suitably informed by the values of what sounds like the ultimate post-Blair triangulating nightmare of 'Red Toryism', a case of 'Colour Me Beautiful' if ever there was one! This seemingly oxymoronic 'big idea' is championed by a working class theologian called Phillip Blond (who happens to be the real-life step-brother of Daniel Craig, aka James Bond) and his new and well-funded (for three years, anyway) think-tank, ResPublica. The right has no monopoly on 'think-tanking' and even the period of quite centrist politics, personified by Blair and Brown, was preceded by intense activity on the part of influential, left-leaning think-tanks like the Institute for Public Policy Research (IPPR) and Demos. Interestingly, these are now 'reaching out' to Tories in a manner that may indicate the current direction of the political wind in the UK.

CONCLUSION

From the way in which I have characterised the UK experience of think-tanks it might seem that I do not take these bodies very seriously: that is not the case. I think that they perform a useful catalytic function that links the world of ideas to the world itself. They might also function pontifically to allow good ideas that are developed in the academy (through research and publishing of various kinds) to travel beyond that space and become 'translated' into action and change by political processes. That is not to say that many academics should be seconded to think-tanks or to political parties, but a more developed think-tank sector, one that engages seriously with politics and public policy and draws on the intellectual capital available nationally and internationally, would at least provide a space in which public intellectualism could flourish. Academics would surely have something to contribute to this.

This may be of minimal utility by way of response to the current 'crisis' but it might help to anticipate future crises with a view to avoiding them or minimising their impact. It might also allow for a democratic amplification of ideas—good and bad—resulting in more informed decision-making that is grounded on a healthier respect for the value of creative and critical thinking. Who knows, it might even allow for some real added value.

'The corporate, managerial vocabulary that is used instead of rhetoric by modern universities and their intellectual leaders…is dreadful. It is idiotic. It is also illiterate and there is more and more of it every year. It's not just the market, the financial market that is in freefall. The language market is in freefall. People are losing the ability to speak. George Orwell is more and more relevant every minute but George Orwell as a horrible comedy rather than a horrible tragedy.'

TOM GARVIN

'The results of privatisation over the last two decades are manifest in the cultural contradictions we have heard about today. An Ireland which is still not sure of whether it is European or American and whose intellects oscillate easily between oppositionism and con-formism, between social critique and private art.'

DECLAN KIBERD

'Public intellectuals become influential, they become really public, in quite specific settings at times when political order and moral certain-ties are shaken. Or when institutions are new or when they are in decay, in for example pre-revolutionary Ireland, or in Ireland in the 1950s as we have heard from Tom Garvin this afternoon, or in South Africa in the 1980s.'

TOM LODGE

THE ASSAULT ON INTELLECTUALISM IN IRISH HIGHER EDUCATION

Tom Garvin

Emeritus Professor of Politics, University College Dublin

INTRODUCTION

In independent Ireland, in times of tranquillity, intellectuals are dispensed with. The views of economists,
novelists, playwrights, sociologists, historians, political
scientists and thoughtful civil servants are dismissed or
ignored. In good times, the warnings of academic economists are denigrated. Once, calamity had people fleeing to
the arms of Mother Church or moving statues of the Virgin
rather than seeking the advice of lay intellectuals. This kind
of miracle-seeking is not quite extinct even now. It was not
until the 1950s that political calamity provoked, and got
popular acceptance for, the advice of established intellectuals. This was, of course, the group containing T.K.
Whitaker, Seán Lemass, a number of civil servants, a few
liberal priests and some academics. Years of reliance on
oracular knowledge from bishops and political ideologues
were suddenly replaced, in September 1957, by a beautiful
young woman, dressed as Ireland, telling a fortune teller
to 'Get to work! They're saying I have no future!' This
cartoon on the cover of *Dublin Opinion*, a humorous
journal, prompted Whitaker to write *Economic Development*
(1958), eventually published by the Irish government

under his name. A youth movement of intellectuals called Tuairim flourished in the late 1950s and 1960s to some considerable impact, but faded away with the coming of television. It appears that intellectuals of the liberal variety are only valued when things have become unstuck.

USEFUL INTELLECTUALS ONLY

The same thing can be seen happening today, provoked again by economic crisis, driven by a mixture of carelessness, greed and disregard for ordinary social intelligence. In recent history, we have seen a desperate political leadership break away from the usual semi-automatic pattern of appointing people from the governmental apparatus to key political posts. Patrick Honohan, a distinguished economist and at one time one of the few employees of the World Bank permitted to live outside the United States, now heads up the Irish Central Bank, thus disrupting the pre-existing apostolic succession to this position by the general secretary of the Department of Finance. Similarly, Colm McCarthy, unusual among Irish economists by being an insider in Irish government, became the moving force behind An Bord Snip Nua. John FitzGerald of the Economic and Social Research Institute (ESRI) is listened to respectfully when he comments on the irresponsibility of much of Irish government's administrative policies: particularly the vote-hunting programme of decentralising civil servants, which has served to wreck the social services system, while also increasing its cost to the taxpayer. Opportunism before critical intelligence has been the usual rule.

LIBERAL AND THEREFORE USELESS INTELLECTUALS

The fate of the Irish intellectual and the creative writer after independence was pretty horrendous. As Frank

O'Connor eloquently put it in 1962, the Irish book censorship system managed to produce a situation in which an entire generation of young people had no knowledge of the literature of their own country. Education in independent Ireland was strangled by vested interests and, by 1955, scientific education in particular lagged far behind such education in 1910. Things improved in the 1960s, with the advent of mass education, as well as a renewed emphasis on vocational education and training for the modern world. However, this welcome shift was accomplished at the expense of the humanist classical and literary curriculum that the better clerical-run high schools had traditionally supplied to a privileged minority. Even levels of literacy in the English language suffered, half-educated 'educationalists' engineering the abolition of grammar and spelling training as being anti-creative.

The value of education, as distinct from practical training for earning one's living, has never been fully grasped in independent Ireland. Much as the British establishment is thought to hate grammar schools, the Irish establishment seems to hate the fee-paying schools that are their equivalent. Rhetoric, literary knowledge, foreign languages and history are commonly, if covertly, regarded as unnecessary or pretentious. This has manifested itself in many ways: for example, it appears that debating societies in many colleges are going into eclipse, partly because of a lack of official sympathy for them. If the present trend continues, it is likely to result in the loss of a whole free-thinking student tradition, much as mediaeval studies and classical studies have been smothered. Furthermore, few will be aware of what has been lost.

The first role of the public intellectual is to encourage or even force people to think. In my time, the most effec-

tive Irish public intellectual was certainly Conor Cruise O'Brien. Educated in a humanist tradition, O'Brien could come up with some hare-brained ideas, but he was adept at rubbing Irish people's noses in unwelcome facts of Irish life, and breaking the silences that characterised much of Ireland's political culture. Easily his biggest contribution to Irish politics was *States of Ireland* (1972), a polemic published at the beginning of the Northern Troubles. The book tore to pieces the lack of realism that lay behind much of Irish public discourse on the reunification of Ireland, the legitimacy of the IRA's 'freedom struggle' and the country's ambivalent relationship with the United Kingdom. He became a hate figure for some, while many others quietly agreed with much of what he said. The key fact is, however, that the book made a difference, and a considerable portion of his thesis was tacitly accepted and used, without acknowledgement, as a basis for a politics of reconciliation. Charlie MacCreevy famously described O'Brien as being like a lighthouse on a bog: brilliant but useless. Though witty, this is untrue; liberal the Cruiser may have been, but scarcely useless.

THE USELESSNESS OF FREE INQUIRY AND THE LEADERSHIP OF IRISH UNIVERSITIES

Andreas Hess wrote with some eloquence in 2009 about a central problem in modern universities—the perceived commerce-driven loss of respect for what is termed 'blue-sky research' or, more cheekily, idle curiosity. One of the human race's greatest inventions, the university, has at its core the free exercise of trained curiosity by intelligent and well-educated people. It appears that many universities are under pressure to engage in applied, intellectually derivative and profitable research at the expense of free enquiry. Intellectual derivativeness is a symptom of provincialism. Great universities do not have this problem, their prestige and endowments protect them, but more humble, if worthy, universities that are being pushed by commercial forces into intellectual provincialism do suffer. Ireland exhibits this problem in an intense form. Researchers are required by bureaucrats and financial controllers to specify what it is that they are going to discover, before the money to do the research is made available. Pablo Picasso's comment is appropriate: 'If you know exactly what you are going to do then what is the point in doing it?'

This notion of 'free research' has come to be regarded as self-indulgent and pointless. The idea of knowledge being an end in itself has become alien to much of elite opinion, and a further *central* belief, that having an appetite for knowledge as a good in itself actually encourages detached and penetrating thinking about very practical matters, is being lost. The real cost of this has been immense, because the result is a loss of wisdom. This entails the growth of silliness and the destruction of imagination. Much of our present crisis could be attributed to such silliness. The opinion, though never possessed by some, that the appetite for knowledge is a positive thing has always existed in Ireland, despite traditional hostility from some governmental and ecclesiastical sources. The connected idea that intellectual leadership should be in the hands of the most accomplished is also being flung away by universities. The universities' leaders imagine they are abolishing self-indulgence, but they are actually blowing out their own brains. We are treated to the spectacle of veterans in modern languages, medieval studies, economic history, engineering, economics, agriculture,

Tom Garvin

Celtic studies or political science being told how to conduct their teaching, research and publication by means that are sometimes wildly inappropriate for the nature of their subjects.

Imposing on these subjects a research model that is derived from the physical sciences stultifies research in languages, history, political science, sociology and the policy sciences in general. This includes economics, the subject our government rather hopes will get us all out of the trouble that deeply anti-intellectual foolishness got us into. The role model put forward is the Chinese university system, created by one of the most hideous regimes of this century. Chinese universities are well-known for their academic feudalism, intellectual plagiarism and hatred of free speech. In 2010 Liu Xiaobo, a famous Chinese dissident who was imprisoned for eleven years for speaking his mind, won the Nobel Peace Prize for his political courage: an enraged Chinese government immediately locked up his wife in her own house. The Chinese government disobeys its own laws while accusing peaceful protestors of disobeying Chinese law. In UCD there is a thing called the Confucius Institute, which obtained seed funding from Beijing and teaches basic Chinese and tai chi. There is another of these things in Cork. A British study of these institutes in Britain reports that they teach a biased version of Chinese history; Confucian education was illegal in China under communist rule for a generation. The study concludes:

> The Chinese government's decision to establish Confucius Institutes in 10 British universities raises several serious questions. By accepting money from the Chinese gov-

ernment, British universities are overlooking the country's human rights record and lack of democracy. In addition, there are concerns that universities which accept Chinese money will feel less able to criticise Chinese policy. There is also reason to believe that the Chinese government is using British universities to advance its foreign policy goals—ironically through funding a subject which the British government has designated as being "strategically important". Furthermore there are fears that the Confucius Institutes portray a disproportionately positive version of China through its teaching (Simcox, 2009, p. 133, passim).

All this is increasingly known internationally. In early 2009, the Labour Court condemned attempts in Trinity College Dublin to limit intellectual freedom and research choices among lecturers and professors in favour of commercial considerations. This decision went under-reported in the Irish papers, but was described by the *Times Higher Education Supplement* as a decision that would echo around the world. There has been a substitution of ranking for one's own informed intellectual judgement in senior management. The results are worthy of Swift's Academy of Projectors in *Gulliver's travels*. It has been proposed by Europe, in effect, that three articles in some unread 'learned' journal controlled by some cabal should be worth more than Keith Thomas' magisterial *Religion and the decline of magic*, or Jared Diamond's classic *Guns, germs and steel*. Einstein wouldn't get hired as professor of physics by this confederacy. The London *Times* comments on this kind of exercise:

> Government adores its faulty league tables of schools, universities, hospitals and local authority services. Instead of intelligent inspection and help, billions of pounds and years of effort are poured into lists and tables that serve little purpose. They demoralise some, make others smug, and condition thousands of managers to work to targets that skew and corrupt their core mission (Purves, 2009).

As Hess (2009) observed, the 'intellectual consequences of this intellectual [*sic*] revolution are disastrous'. Furthermore, this government-driven assault on Irish intellectual life, apparently initiated by politicians, has been met with a deafening silence by Irish journalism. Why? John Kelly (2009) has urged the government to assert its authority over higher education. He is right in pointing to the anti-intellectualism of the universities' rulers, but is chanting at the wrong spook.

This assault on intellectual life is being financed by our taxes, and it should be dawning on government that one of its most valuable assets, the third-level education system, has been taken over by non-academic forces. The universities are our collective brains, and contempt for them is stupid and unpatriotic. The people who 'run' Irish universities pretend to be businessmen running efficient enterprises. They also pretend that their activities are going to bring about greater economic growth: this is false, and there is evidence that education beyond secondary level has no obvious connection with growth; this holds particularly for small countries where there is a local capacity to import higher education. Anti-intellectualism automatically leads to the glorification of ignorance, and Ireland is well on the way from the former to the latter.[1]

‘It is the patent failure of the concept of regulation that we keep talking about. We are dependent on regulation to deliver on a whole set of instruments…There is a fantasy land out there in a whole area of regulation where we are encouraged to believe that the regulator is fine, doing the job, and I think that's a huge weakness. The present crisis is directly related to that not just in Ireland, but globally.'

FRANCES RUANE

‘We should be careful in distinguishing between the role that public intellectuals play in developing critical thinking and debate and enriching the conceptual vocabulary at the disposal of citizens and the role they may play as technocratic experts. And I don't think they play that latter role usefully.'

TOM LODGE

‘The job of public intellectuals is to make the powers that be uneasy in their beds. My own belief is that this is a more appropriate role for intellectuals. This is the tradition of Sartre and Simone de Beauvoir which in fact was inherited in North America by Edward Said. He talked about the intellectual as an amateur speaking truth to power.'

DECLAN KIBERD

PUBLIC INTELLECTUALS IN TIMES OF CRISIS: THE ROLE OF ACADEMIA

Frances Ruane

Economic and Social Research Institute

INTRODUCTION

In 2001 Richard Posner, US Appeals Court judge, wrote a major book entitled *Public intellectuals: a study of decline*. In the book, he drew attention to the evolution of public intellectuals over the past century and the fact that today most of them hold academic positions. As a consequence, the role and focus of the intellectual in public debate is influenced by what is happening in the world of academe. Posner reflects on how the development of academic scholarship over the twentieth century has seen an increase in specialisation, as scholars in most disciplines focus their time more deeply within a sub-discipline rather than widely within the general discipline. (Research for Posner's book involved data analysis of media mentions, Web hits and scholarly citations of public intellectuals in the US from 1995–2000). Consequently, according to Posner (2001), the potential role of academics as public intellectuals is disappearing—they simply do not have the skill-sets to engage in critical commentary about the world in which they live.

But what happens in a time of crisis, and particularly a time of economic crisis, when the issues are new and complex? What role could or should the academic economist, for instance, play in a society that is not just threatened by the crisis itself but fearful that a lack of understanding of the key issues may contribute further to the crisis? If economists engage in public analysis of the crisis, how will that impact on their personal standing in the future, and the standing of economists generally? Could they contribute to the crisis by what they say and how they say it? (For instance, there were accusations that the ESRI's (2008) Quarterly Economic Commentary actually caused the economic crisis, by stating that Ireland was in recession.) Is it usually the case that academics are prepared to engage in discussion when they have done the relevant research, or, at least, when others have conducted the research and they are very familiar with it? For example, Morgan Kelly's (2007) analysis of how the housing price spiral would end, based on international literature about similar bubbles in other markets, indicated that soft landings following this scale of spiral simply did not occur in practice. Unfortunately, the recent crisis has not allowed for the luxury of research, and it is clear that engagement can only be on the basis of heavy caveats, which are not generally part of the public discourse in economics. In effect, while the language of economists has tended to be definitive for the past number of decades, the present crisis has opened up an entirely new situation which merits a different rhetoric, especially when interacting with the wider public. One of Posner's criticisms of his fellow academics in the US—namely, their careless use of evidence when speaking publicly—is especially relevant now, in a time of crisis.

While many others have written on this topic in the past decade, this paper will draw on Posner's framework, since it is particularly suited to examining economists in the public domain (in addition to legal research, Posner has contributed to economics through his work in competition). Using this framework, this paper reflects on how Irish academics have interacted in public debate and in the media since the onset of the current economic crisis. It explores the factors that impact generally on the participation of academics in public debates, and then more particularly on how the participation of Irish academic economists has been affected by the recent crisis. This discussion is set in the context of how the media itself has changed over the past decade.

THE ROLES OF PUBLIC INTELLECTUALS

To provide some distance from current issues, it is perhaps helpful to distinguish, in general terms, three types of engagement that academics have with the wider public:

• engagement that involves the academics presenting insights to the public into the complexity of a given discipline in which developments are of profound importance. In effect, the wider public is given an understanding of a discipline which may interest them but which they have not previously had the opportunity to study. In the scientific area, names like Stephen Hawkins and Richard Feynman come to mind. In economics, Amartya Sen's book *Development as freedom* is an example of this type of engagement. Such knowledge will be referred to as 'complex knowledge';

• engagement whereby public intellectuals tease out some of the links between their own discipline and the wider context beyond it—in effect, connecting their specialism with a broader disciplinary environment. In economics, this can take the form of examining the implications of research for developing policy. This role has gained importance in recent decades as academic research has become increasingly specialised. Indeed, sub-disciplinary specialism is now the norm. The potential loss through specialisation has been recognised and underpins the increased promotion of multidisciplinary research to connect both sub-disciplines and wider disciplines. This is evident in the establishment of institutes and funding grants that require the involvement of multidisciplinary teams. In a sense, the role of the public intellectual in this context mirrors what is happening within the Academy. Steven Weinberg is someone who currently plays this role in the field of physics, while Milton Friedman is well known for having drawn on his research to influence the development of monetary policy. This will be referred to below as 'cross-connection knowledge';

• engagement by public intellectuals who write and speak across a range of public issues outside the discipline in which they have earned their academic stripes. The authority of these public intellectuals emanates from their position rather than their knowledge or scholarship in the areas that they discuss. In other words, people listen to them because of who they are rather than what they know about a particular issue. Posner (2001) sees this type of engagement as potentially undermining the role of academics because they do not have the requisite knowledge about the area they are addressing. He cites examples of public intellectuals (including the economist Paul Krugman) who, in his view, use research from outside their own discipline without adequate care. On the global stage, many Nobel laureates have to resist being propelled into this role by media pressure to speak outside their areas of specialism and even outside their own disciplines. Most listings of public intellectuals (and many exist on the web) cite Noam Chomsky as the leading public intellectual in the world. He undoubtedly fits into this category of public intellectual, attracting particularly large audiences when talking about major areas of public concern, rather than linguistics. This will be referred to as 'general knowledge'.

Finally, in addition to this three-part framework (complex knowledge, cross-connection knowledge and general knowledge), it is possible for academics to operate outside of their own fields of specialisation without risk, if they use their theoretical knowledge to question rather than to inform. Thus, without knowing the specifics of the areas, the academic can add to the debate by identifying necessary questions. In the recent crisis, one valuable contribution made by academics has been to help identify what we do not know, what we can not know and what we should be able to find out. According to Poser's framework, this would not strictly constitute playing the role of a public intellectual.

IRISH ACADEMIC ECONOMISTS IN A TIME OF CRISIS

How does this three-part framework help us to consider the contributions of academic economists in the current crisis?

To understand the present situation, the general public has sought 'complex knowledge' of the issues relating to banking, which would not previously have been of interest. For example, terms like 'sub-prime lending' and 'subordinated debt', which are now widely used in the media, would not, in the early days of the crisis, have formed part of the popular vocabulary in Ireland or elsewhere. In these early days it was important that academics, particularly finance experts, and other key professionals (for example banking analysts not working within the banks themselves) played their role as providers of this information. Their independence, their in-depth knowledge, and the authority they carried based on that knowledge were crucial in the light of the perceived loss of trust in information emanating from the banks themselves. This was especially so as economists in the private sector, especially in the banks, were the most regular contributors to media discussions and debates on the economy in the decade prior to 2008. This high level of private sector participation in the media reflected both a willingness to engage (because of the value of brand recognition in the media) and the ability of these economists to communicate effectively to a general audience. In the beginning of the current crisis, academics became the key source of this 'complex knowledge', displacing their private sector counterparts who had dominated in the boom. As time has gone on, this role has become less necessary as media commentators and others are now familiar with these complex concepts.

A key feature of the recession has been the need for 'cross-connection knowledge' at two levels. At the research level, the consequences of increased specialism had to be addressed, with research in different areas being interconnected in order to understand and analyse the full complexity of the crisis. Examples include: the connection between macro economics, monetary policy and banking regulation; the connection between the banking crisis and the fiscal crisis; and the connection between the housing market and credit markets. The research agendas in many areas have evolved and adapted to address these new and complex issues. At the public engagement level, there has been exceptional pressure on economists to explain these cross-connections as part of real-time commentary on the crisis. However, since the complexities are still being researched, engagement with the anxious public poses high risks to those participating. They may turn out to be wrong, and consequently pilloried in the media and elsewhere. In the Irish context, very few economists were equipped to operate in this arena. Those who have done so since the beginning of the crisis have gone beyond the role of providing knowledge, and have played the cross-connection role of the public intellectual by seeking to suggest on the basis of their analysis what 'should be done'.

For economists whose research lies outside those areas relevant to the crisis, there were pressures to use their 'general knowledge' to opine on the issues of the day. For example, in autumn 2009 there were two instances where visitors were asked to comment on the 'Irish situation' which was outside their areas of expertise. In a radio interview, David (Danny) Blanchflower advised that 'Ireland should now adopt a counter-cyclical fiscal policy' without understanding the context, namely, that the country had an exploding debt burden due to having run pro-cyclical policies for the previous fifteen years. In a television interview in the same month, Noam Chomsky responded to a question about what Ireland should do in the face of the current crisis, saying: 'I would not give advice without knowing a lot about what is happening—and I don't know enough'. This intense need by the media and the public to comprehend a crisis is understandable, but for the most part academic economists have avoided being pushed into this role, leaving it to their macro/finance colleagues. Where they have ventured an answer, most have done so using questioning, rather than definitive, language. Perhaps one long term effect of this crisis is to promote among the general public a better understanding of the intra-disciplinary differences between areas of economics.

ACADEMICS AND JOURNALISTS

Another issue deserving attention is where the interface lies between the role of the academic and the media specialist—and this refers to the economic journalist. A simple characterisation of the academic is one with narrow, specialist interests—the key to publication in peer-reviewed journals and promotion—who takes at minimum a 'medium term' horizon (five years) in planning research. The journalist, on the other hand, has to remain a generalist (especially in a small country such as Ireland) and must operate to a far stricter timetable where an hour constitutes 'short term' and 'long term' is a week.

These characterisations have been altered somewhat by the crisis. It has realigned academics' focus in a more generalist direction, as the issues that arise no longer fit neatly into the pigeon holes of the international literature. It is too early yet to measure what overall impact the crisis has had on the research agendas of Irish economists but it seems likely that the resulting issues will become increasingly evident in future research outputs. In any event, the changed state of the economy has raised a range of new issues and it remains to be seen whether or not Irish economists will engage in research that reflects those profound changes. Already there is some evidence of this in the creation of a policy section in the *Economic and Social Review*, the leading Irish journal in economics. The papers for this section reflect both direct and indirect policy issues raised by the crisis and are peer reviewed to a very tight schedule.

In this sense, the time horizon has been shortened some-what, as academic publications have, generally, not been unduly concerned hitherto with any issue of immediacy.

As well as impacting on research, the crisis has affected the relevant academics that have had to follow events more closely and be available to comment on them in public far more than before, when this was seen largely as the domain of the private sector economists. (This is in marked contrast to over a decade of consensus, where the views of even modest contrarians were not sought.) The academics have concentrated on contributing to 'high-level' media and going head to head on TV programmes, meeting the desire of TV producers to host debates among experts. Increasingly, there is a distinction between two types of debates on television—debate among experts on the one hand, and debate among politicians and represen-tatives of social partnership on the other. Debate is also back on the agenda in 'virtual' form: primarily through the Irish Economy Blog [www.irisheconomy.ie], which was set up in the very early days of the crisis. The blog suffers from the limitation associated with public debate, as compared with academically rigorous debate, in that the content is not subject to any refereeing process. The quality of the debate, therefore, is dependent on the knowledge and analysis of the participants.[1]

For economic journalists, there have also been some changes. Access to global knowledge has changed dramat-ically with the development of the Internet, and journalists are much less dependent on having direct contact with local experts as a result. The numerous eco-nomic blogs, including the Irish Economy Blog, are also major sources of material. One positive feature of such blogs is that they expose the journalist to a variety of view-points—consensus is one attribute that could not be ascribed to most debates on the Irish Economy Blog and there certainly is no 'culture of consensus' apparent. The journalists draw explicitly on named experts as a method of giving their coverage credibility, rather than necessarily as a source of information.[2] In effect, the economic journalists now have more access to 'real time' economic arguments than ever before, further reducing the time horizon in which they operate.

At the same time, several journalists have chosen to contribute in longer time frameworks by writing books about the crisis that are aimed at the public, meeting a need that academic economists show no interest in filling.[3] They also have become more specialised, with articles and programmes being devoted to quite narrow subject fields. In the case of newspapers, this has been accompanied by much better use of graphics which can contribute very significantly to enhancing clarity on the issues involved. On television, there has been a strong emphasis on visualising the crisis (bank buildings, deserted office blocks, vast empty housing estates, stock exchange floors, etc), with voice-overs to provide a more technical discussion of the issues. It is not clear how costly such visuals are but at times it may be the case that they leave too little time for real debate. For example, the typical Prime Time programme seems to work to a formula of a dramatic-sounding introduction, followed by dramatic (and often repetitive) visuals interspersed with sound bites, with a relatively short studio debate on the key issues coming afterwards.

The roles of the economic journalists and economists overlapped to some extent during the crisis but this should not continue to be the case. The requirement for journalists to produce short-term copy and a flow of fresh news/ideas is completely at variance with the role of academics. A new harmony must be found in which the role of the academic economist as a public intellectual becomes more reflective and less preoccupied with real-time commentating.

CONCLUSION

As we move on from the crisis, the demand for academics in Ireland to engage in public discussions on the crisis will inevitably recede. The requirement for expertise to inform the public has already reduced and the knowledge of the economic journalists has increased, thereby reducing the call on the specialist economists for 'complex knowledge'. There will be a continuing and possibly increasing call on researchers to provide 'cross-connecting knowledge' insights as the economy starts on a recovery path. Can anything now be said about the contribution of Irish economists in the crisis, and whether it can have any lasting effect?

In terms of willingness to engage with the public during the crisis, Irish economists were not found lacking. Their eagerness to engage is reflected in the growth of the Irish Economy Blog—one public medium where people could contribute without invitation. It is also reflected in the increase in opinion pieces, contributions to live media and seminars for the wider public.[4]

The crisis has certainly reconnected the economics profession with the economy, as it has done with the entire academic community. The bubble contributed to a dulling of debate about economic and social issues as academic economists quite rationally focused their attention on journal publications in the face of policy-making that steadfastly ignored any evidence they produced. This, and the openness of debate on the economy, is something that will hopefully change permanently as we move on. Had academic economists walked away from the analysis of the crisis an opportunity would have been missed but to their credit, they did not.

6

'It seems to me that the public sphere has been abandoned by all kinds of people, among them intellectuals, among them academics. I think what emerged through the afternoon is the truth that an academic is not necessarily an intellectual, and an intellectual is not necessarily an academic but that's okay. Some critical mass of academics have made a contribution as public intellectuals in the past. If that number drops below a level of critical mass, it isn't just society that suffers—and society does suffer—it is academia itself.'

DECLAN KIBERD

9

'Public intellectuals need a constituency to function within, a public which shares a sense of community and a public which is eager to engage with discursive thinking—disciplined, systematic, difficult thinking about important issues. These publics don't always exist.'

TOM LODGE

6

'I think it's a culture. The message is that there are no consequences for the abuse of power unless you are at the bottom. And our culture, organisationally, nationally legitimates that and I think that is what we can learn.'

PAT O'CONNOR

9

REFLECTIONS ON THE PUBLIC INTELLECTUAL'S ROLE IN A GENDERED SOCIETY

Pat O'Connor

Department of Sociology, University of Limerick

PUBLIC INTELLECTUALS:
DEFINITION AND POSSIBILITIES

The word 'intellectuals' is used by Miliband (1982) 'to denote the people who are mainly concerned with the formation, articulation and dissemination of ideas' (p. 87). Gramsci (1971) suggests that everyone can be an intellectual, but that not everyone in society 'has the function of intellectuals' (p. 9). Implicit in Gramsci's ideas about intellectuals is a concern with ideology and the ways in which ideas and systems of ideas are used by the powerful to present social arrangements as 'natural', 'inevitable', and 'what people want'. He also refers to the existence of traditional intellectuals (such as teachers and academics, judges and lawyers) and questions their impartiality.

O'Dowd (1996) argues that Irish intellectuals were traditionally preoccupied with national identity and with '"constructing" or "imagining" the nation' (p. 16). In an increasingly consumerist society, they became 'the "professionals", the bureaucrats, the producers and distributors of "culture", well paid but politically irrelevant' (p. 20).

O'Dowd suggests that the relationship between intellectuals and power bases in Irish society, including 'class, institutional, political and gender dimensions', was typically ignored (p. 7). It is now glaringly obvious that the market and consumerism are no longer sufficient as sources of meaning or identity, and that the political and moral role of intellectuals under these circumstances is very relevant.

Various methods of categorising intellectuals have been put forward. Burawoy (2005) identifies four types of knowledge, each of which potentially has a public aspect (O'Connor, 2006). Implicit in each of these four types is the concept of a 'public intellectual':

• critical knowledge, concerned with challenging taken-for-granted ideas and reflecting an underlying commitment to a 'better world';

• policy-oriented knowledge, which attempts to provide policy solutions and, in particular, hold the state publicly accountable;

• knowledge emerging from and concerned with a dialogue with the public around relevant issues;

• knowledge about methods and the conceptual frameworks available to those interested in the scientific status of the knowledge.

There are always contradictions in our accepted views of the world, 'that can be exploited for ideological challenge and resistance' (Baker, Lynch, Cantillon & Walsh, 2009, p. 215). Some intellectuals, because of their background or attitude to power, can demystify these views that are taken for granted and 'construct new forms of discourse through which effective opposition and critical expression can be achieved' (Ransome, 1992, p. 196). Thus, they identify choices that might otherwise be ignored because they constitute 'a latent or manifest challenge to the values or interests of the decision maker' (quoted in Lukes, 1974, p. 44).

It has been suggested that: 'If the intellectual wishes to understand the society in which he lives, he has only one course open to him and that is to adopt the point of view of its most underprivileged members' (Sartre, 1974, p. 255). The night of the banking crisis in September 2008 and the subsequent decision to create the National Asset Management Agency (NAMA) involved intensive consultation between the government and the bankers. Who adopted the perspective of the underprivileged, and considered the impact of these decisions on them? The impact on women has attracted even less attention (despite the exemplary work of agencies such as the National Women's Council). Indeed, the state's endorsement of neo-liberal capitalist policies meant it had, to a certain extent, women to thank for the creation of the Celtic Tiger, though little concern was shown for the ultimate impact it has had on women's lives (O'Hagan, 2009), and the same can be said for its demise.

Theoretically, public intellectuals can be seen as being concerned with creating new agendas and raising issues that those in power currently wish to avoid. They can also be seen as concerned with transforming what Wright Mills (1970) called 'private troubles' into 'public issues'. Thus, for example, public intellectuals might be preoccupied with raising issues about the appropriateness of a total focus on the market (to the exclusion of society); about the extent to which the current social and political arrangements (including distributions of wealth) are inevitable or about the idea that gender is now irrelevant since 'equality is a *fait accompli'* (Ging, 2009).

WHAT IS MEANT BY 'TIMES OF CRISIS'?

In Ireland, we are all acutely aware of a banking crisis, a wider economic crisis, a political crisis and an unemployment crisis. Underlying these is a crisis concerning the power of the market and its relationship with the state— and ultimately the priority given to the creation of private wealth over all other social or economic objectives (Cronin, Kirby & Ging 2009). In the future in Ireland, it seems clear that poverty will continue to increase and long-term unemployment and civil unrest will be realities. There will be an even greater lack of trust of those in political positions and of those professionals who are thought to be 'in the pay of' organisations that are seen as solely committed to advancing their members' interests. Satires such as Scrap Saturday (an RTÉ Radio One sketch show that ran from 1989–91) problematised the definition of the 'national interest' and everyone enjoyed the joke. Now, faced with ever more revelations involving high-profile people in the context of a deepening economic crisis, the question of the legitimacy of the state's authority is being raised. The fact that the political elite and, indeed, the business elite are male-dominated adds a further filter in terms of their concerns and priorities. We are arguably on the brink of a crisis of legitimacy along class and gender lines. Even before the economic collapse, the legitimacy of institutional power, the overwhelming majority of which was held by men, was in question. Thus, Connell (1987) identified 'a crisis of institutionalisation', reflecting 'a weakening of the ability of the institutional order of family-plus-state to sustain the legitimacy of men's power' (p. 159). Connell suggests that the long-term political source of this is 'generalisable claims to equality' as the basis for the state's legitimacy (p. 160). Large portions of state expenditure (for example investment in women's education) directly or indirectly increase the likelihood of challenges to the legitimacy of male power. There are tensions too arising from the ongoing patriarchal nature of the Irish political system, where geographical representation is seen as essential and unproblematic but where the issue of women's representation by men is seen as unproblematic and warrants no public discussion.

Gender as an issue in Irish society today includes poverty amongst women—especially women who are lone parents—and the difficulties experienced, particularly by women, in combining paid work and family responsibilities in a society where women still carry the main responsibility for housework and child-care (Lynch & Lyons, 2008). Women experience 'glass ceilings' and homosocial organisational cultures in male-dominated organisations, with sizeable proportions of those who have been successful in such organisations reporting discrimination and prejudice (Humphreys, Drew & Murphy, 1999; O'Connor, 1996, 2010). We know that, per hour, women still earn less than men (86 per cent per hour: see Russell, McGinnity, Callan & Keane, 2009, p. 45). We know that, even amongst young graduates in the public sector, patterns of differential privileging of men and women are apparent within the first five years (Russell, Smyth & O'Connell, 2005), and that these patterns are even more pronounced in the private sector. Gendered patterns persist, unnoticed, even within family life (where boys are likely to get more pocket money than girls

(McCoy & Smyth, 2004) and are less likely to undertake domestic chores (Leonard, 2004)). The underperformance of boys compared to girls in education is seen by the state, the education system and the media as reflecting the inadequacies of the education system, while the achievements of middle-class children, as compared to working-class children, are seen as reflecting their greater ability. Thus, in contrast to the class-based message, there has been no attempt to encourage boys to emulate the strong work ethic, deference, diligence and achievement orientation involved in 'doing girl' (Clancy, 2001; Lynch & Lodge, 2002). Why do you think that is?

In the public discourses generated by the state, educational institutions and, frequently, the media, gender patterns are simultaneously assumed to exist and are denied since they are seen as reflecting essentialist and immutable realities, which are not amenable to state intervention (Ging, 2009). Thus, existing measures of economic growth (Gross National Product (GNP)/Gross Domestic Product (GDP)) under-estimate women's contribution by excluding unpaid work in the home (thus effectively ignoring 25–40 per cent) on the grounds of technical difficulty, although this has long been challenged (Fahey, 1990). Similarly, during the Celtic Tiger period, construction (an area of predominantly male employment) became a particular focus for state support, rather than, for example, nursing services (an area of predominantly female employment), arguably reflecting gendered prioritisation (O'Connor, 2008c). Such patterns need to be located in the context of a society where the political system remains male-dominated and clientelistic, and hence one where politicians may be more likely to respond to lobbies from the construction industry than from nursing services. However, in a context where two-thirds of those in employment are in the service sector, and where the export of traded services is a potentially major source of international revenue, the export of nursing services is an area where Ireland might have a competitive advantage. Yet this was not even considered, whereas domestic construction was seen as an obvious focus for state support, arguably reflecting the 'habitus' (Bourdieu, 1977, pp. 82–83) of many of those involved in state policy and in the education system who grew to manhood when the Marriage Bar (O'Connor, 1998) was in existence. Interestingly, the area in which women are most likely to be in senior positions is civic society and the organisations related to it. Women constitute the majority of those heading Community Development Projects in disadvantaged areas, whether as programme co-ordinators or as chairs of the voluntary management committees (O'Dowd, 2009). Interestingly, such pro-grammes were early targeted for cutting.

The 2007–11 Fianna Fáil-led coalition government was consistently and actively disinterested in gender equality. It fused the Department of Equality and Law Reform with the far larger and more conservative Department of Justice in 1997 (O'Connor, 2008c) and in 2008 imposed a cut of 42 per cent in the Equality Authority's budget, at a time when cuts of 9 per cent were being imposed elsewhere. It showed no willingness to ensure that proportionate gender representation exists in the political system. It was less than assiduous in implementing the state's 40 per cent gender balance recommendation as regards the composition of boards in key areas.

There are fundamental tensions at the heart of Irish culture today. We have lost faith in the traditional source of moral control, the institutional Roman Catholic Church. We are becoming an increasingly individualised society of 'me and mine', whether 'mine' is defined in terms of family, class-based friendships or political tribes. The valorisation of the market dominates public discourse, endorsed by the state, and it has begun to impact on higher-education institutions. The fact that, through NAMA and the Special Purpose Vehicle, we are effectively transferring massive resources from the tax-payer to organisations (i.e. banks), which are staffed at the top predominantly by those who have brought about the collapse and whose main responsibility is to increase private profits, raises fundamental questions about the future of the state and its legitimacy in the eyes of the public.

To summarise, in addition to the commonly identified crises, there is the ongoing tendency to see gendered patterns—if they are seen at all—as a reflection of biological reality and beyond the responsibility of any structure. Beneath this kind of thinking, arguably, lie fantasies about a return to a male breadwinner model (a fantasy that sits uneasily with the fact that 43 per cent of the female labour force has third-level qualifications: Russell *et al.*, 2009). In a context characterised by a decline in confidence in both the market and the state, an ethos of 'looking after your own' may constitute some kind of a positive lever if the definition of 'your own' is extended by public intellectuals to include all Irish citizens.

WHAT FACILITATES THE DEVELOPMENT OF PUBLIC INTELLECTUALS?

In a sense, the most obvious place to look for public intellectuals is in the universities because of their role in the creation and transmission of knowledge. And yet, in many ways, universities are problematic sites for such intellectuals, partly because of the current perceived nature and purpose of education and the kinds of structures that facilitate it.

It has been suggested that 'universities have been transformed increasingly into powerful consumer-oriented corporate networks, whose public interest values have been seriously challenged' (Lynch *et al.*, 2009, p. 296; also Sullivan, 2009). Paradoxically, this has been done in the name of increasing their public accountability. However, the patriarchal character of such institutions has been ignored. Gramsci (1971), writing in the 1930s, saw education as a process involving not only the acquisition of specific skills but 'the development of intellectual self discipline and moral independence that enables people to make sense of their own experiences within the broader context of society'. In Wright Mills' (1970) terms, it helps people to see 'private troubles' (whether these are unemployment, poverty, distribution of wealth and privilege, discrimination) as issues that need public action. Lynch *et al.* (2009) suggest that there are many structural and cultural obstacles to universities working this way, including their disciplinary focus and their concern with distancing themselves from normative activities and depicting normative concerns as an unworthy politicisation of knowledge. They argue that universities inhibit the development of critical public intellectuals concerned with challenging taken-for-granted ideas and putting forward conceptions of a 'better world'.

There is a tension between the increasingly specialist nature of knowledge required in universities, and the activity of the public intellectual, whether in critical reflection or public dialogue. Measures of research excellence that rest on assessments made by other professionals (reflected in citation rates mainly generated by international, refereed journal articles), as opposed to broader indicators of societal impact, further undermine connections with the wider society and potentially absolve academics from responsibilities as regards societal transformation. Paradoxically, the result can be that those with no specialist social scientific or humanist knowledge at all are the most comfortable adopting the role of the 'generalist humanistic intellectual addressing a broad social constituency' (O'Dowd, 1996, p. 1).

Although purporting to encourage the public accountability of universities, the state is implicitly fostering a managerial ethos rather than one focused on social justice/human rights issues. One of the features of a managerialist system is the development of executive groups, who, to a large extent, are appointed by and report directly to the president. In that context, there are strong pressures towards homosociability (i.e. presidents appointing people like themselves: Grummell *et al.*, 2009; O'Connor, 2010). Since the majority of the funding for universities is received from the state we have to ask, how likely is it that senior academic management will challenge state policies or actions? Individual factors, such as reluctance to becoming involved in public fora, lack of time, limited leadership capacities and a sense that such activity is not institutionally valued, also exist. Furthermore, even if university-based public intellectuals do emerge, raising of gender-related issues may still be problematic in a situation where the overwhelming majority of those at professorial level (89 per cent) are men; as are the overwhelming majority (82 per cent) of those in senior management positions in the universities. In a recent study

(O'Connor, 2009a; 2010), senior management culture in Irish universities was found to be characterised by male homosociability and conformity.

For Gramsci (1971), each type of economic production creates a stratum of intellectuals, including technical people as well as those that legitimated that kind of economic production politically. Currently, the state is very much concerned with the production of graduates with narrowly defined skill bases, who can facilitate the development of industry today—particularly those in the areas of science and technology (O'Connor, 2008b). The accepted importance of these areas has become the mantra of powerful lobbyists, such as Science Foundation Ireland, and has been reflected in the investment of substantial levels of research funding, focused on potential exports rather than on employment. Even while accepting that scientific or technological ideas are important for economic development, it is by no means clear that innovations in such areas are the exclusive prerogative of science or technology graduates. Nonetheless, education policies seem directed primarily towards producing graduates in particular areas of science and technology—the sustainability of which areas has been questioned (Sheehan, 2005; Jordan & O'Leary, 2007). During 1997–2004, the Celtic Tiger era, some employment sectors identified as experiencing considerable growth were health professionals, teachers, care assistants, financial accountants and clerks, craftsmen, builders, labourers and sales assistants (Turner & D'Art, 2005). It is by no means clear how such areas created a need for university-educated science and technology graduates. Yet state officials and influential intellectuals saw such investment as key (O'Connor, 2008b). If graduates from these areas continue to work in state-funded university projects, the relative cost and benefit of such employment creation needs to be balanced against alternatives. In 2007, an Organisation for Economic Co-operation and Development (OECD) report found that Ireland had the highest child-care costs as a proportion of earnings in the 26 OECD countries—almost a third of the average family's expenditure. State payment for workers in child-care centres would therefore greatly reduce that burden, and equally create employment. Yet this strategy has not even been considered. Nor has there been any consideration of the idea in the National Development Plan's Mid Term Review (Fitzgerald *et al.*, 2005) that, in a knowledge-based society, investment in subjects such as history could be traded internationally just as easily as any other kind of knowledge, with obvious outcomes such as state support for universities to attract international students in such areas.

Baker *et al.* (2009, p. 227) highlight the importance of 'naming and claiming an intellectual space for new narratives in public discourse'. The ability of social scientists to claim that space has long been questioned (Kane, 1996). The absence in Ireland of a clearly defined public arena in which to put forward ideas must be recognised. There has never been an equivalent of the agora and forum of Ancient Greece and Rome: a public space for discussion of ideas. Perhaps the nearest contemporary equivalent is the media, but its audiences are fractured by age, class, gender and region. In the printed media, the 'gatekeepers' (Husu, 2006) are working for commercial entities who have vested interests in the perpetuation of certain taken-for-granted views. Ging (2009) noted that in such outlets 'the broad acceptance of the myth that equality has been achieved... [has] ultimately served to gloss over the substantial material inequalities between men and women' (p. 69). The democ-ratisation of sources, reflected in the development of blogs such as The Irish Economy (www.irisheconomy.ie), does offer interesting possibilities. Indeed, as Baker *et al.* (2009) recognise, blogs are likely to become 'one of the primary engines of change (or resistance to change) in contempo-rary societies' (p. 214).

Organisations such as The Equality Authority of Ireland or the Combat Poverty Agency have been vital in com-missioning research to challenge hegemonic realities, and providing structural contexts to legitimate it. However, this seems unlikely to continue, and independently funded structures such as the Think Tank for Action on Social Change (TASC) may become increasingly important. Given the current economic crisis, space outside the insti-tutional structures will exist, but it seems likely that this will encourage issue-related action, rather than reflection on the power structures and their consequences, and the emergence of Irish pensioners as a power bloc in opposi-tion to the medical card issue was an example of this.

It is very striking that, despite huge economic, social and cultural changes in Irish society, the basic institutional structures and the profiles of those at the top have changed very little in terms of class and gender. It seems reasonable to suggest, therefore, that the culture of priv-ilege and entitlement also remains within them, and that they provide a less than fertile terrain in which to find public intellectuals concerned with problematising such patterns.

SO WHAT CAN PUBLIC INTELLECTUALS OFFER?

Kirby *et al.* (2009) suggest that public intellectuals are important in challenging common sense understandings, in mobilising people within broadly based social movements, and ultimately in impacting on institutional structures. At the most fundamental level, the role of a public intellectual is to question the value premises, power structures and resource allocations of Irish society. Behind it is a more or less explicit version of what can crudely be described as a 'better world'—a world that is at odds with patriarchal and/or class privileging. The work of the School of Social Justice in University College Dublin (Lynch, 1999a, 1999b; Lynch & Lodge, 2002; Baker *et al.*, 2004, 2009) has been particularly concerned with such a normative approach. In a number of universities, including the University of Limerick, gender is seen 'as a fundamental feature of the capitalist system: arguably as fundamental as class divisions. Socialist theory cannot any longer evade the fact that capitalism is run mainly by and to the benefit of men' (Connell, 1995, p. 104). In this context, gender is seen as a property of institutions or processes, with social landscapes being more or less 'mapped' by gender at social, cultural and psychological levels. Thus, despite some similarities in the lives of boys/girls and men/women, an overwhelming amount of the highest political, economic and religious power in western society, for example, is held by men; the majority of unpaid work in the home is still being done by women. Even clothes for young children are still colour coded by gender (blue for a boy, pink for a girl). In Connell's (2002) terms: 'These facts form a pattern which we may call the gender arrangements or 'gender order' of contemporary society' (p. 3). Of course, individuals may reject these 'natural', 'inevitable', 'taken-for-granted' roles, but the key point that Connell is making is that such gendered paths continue to exist. The nature of these paths themselves may, of course, also change over time to reflect wider social, cultural and economic changes. Thus, for example, the dramatic increases in the proportion of female principals in primary schools (Lynch, 1994), in the context of campaigns by the unions and elements in the state, challenged the depiction of gender patterns in this area as 'natural', 'inevitable', and 'what women want'. However the degendering of particular paths co-exist within the overall context of gendered continuity within the educational system—with women constituting the majority of those in primary teaching and men the majority of those in university lecturing, and in executive and senior academic positions within the universities.

So, what can public intellectuals do? Firstly, public intellectuals can challenge the hi-jacking of discourses that facilitate a concern with 'a better world', for example the concept of fairness that is currently being used to justify the cutting of child benefit—a universal benefit paid in recognition of the fact that wages paid to individuals do not take account of the needs of children. This kind of argument raises the question of whether those who do not have children should be favoured over those who do. With child-care costs at €1000 a month in Dublin, are women in paid employment being forced to give up that paid work because they cannot afford to pay for child-care? Parents in Ireland spend roughly 20 per cent of their incomes on child-care (Lynch and Lyons 2008), as compared with an average of eight per cent in other EU countries (McGinnity and Russell, 2008). In effect then parents in Ireland pay up to 90 per cent of their child-care costs in comparison to 33 per cent in Denmark and 20 per cent in Sweden (NYC1, 2010). Is the fact that child benefit is paid to the mother, who is almost always seen as the person responsible for meeting child-care costs, at all relevant to those wishing to cut it? We know that channelling money through the mother increases the likelihood that it will be spent on the children (Rottman, 1994)—is that important in a society where the level of child poverty is already significantly higher than the OECD average (16 per cent versus 12 per cent: McDonough & Loughrey, 2009, p. 3) and likely to increase? The state has long provided tax relief on payments to farm managers who are filling in for farmers, but it has never provided tax relief on child-care. Why not? The argument that it would be fairer to withdraw child benefit from well-off families begs the question about why the taxation system is not used to promote income equality while leaving universal child benefit intact, since it is the only benefit that is paid directly to the mother and it is known that such monies are most likely to be spent on the children. Public intellectuals can play an important role in raising questions about the extent to which policies surrounding child-care reflect patriarchal interests (and indeed implicitly endorse the view that child-care is women's responsibility and is best discharged by the woman withdrawing from the labour force and being financially dependent on her husband/partner).

Next, public intellectuals can mobilise wider community awareness through their own media presence (Vincent Browne's columns in the *Irish Times* on income inequality in Ireland are an excellent example of this). It has been widely recognised that there was a widening of the gap between the incomes of the top and the bottom 10 per cent in the 1990s, with McDonough & Loughrey (2009) showing that income inequality in Ireland was one-third higher than in Sweden or Denmark. Furthermore, although most incomes have decreased since the recession, there is a similar ratio between the incomes of those at the top and the bottom. There have been assertions in the media that 'fairness' was likely to undermine the stability of the state. Implicitly, to suggest that social welfare payments should be cut is simply to legitimate the low pay, gender discrimination and poor pension provision of those at the lowest levels of the private sector. Nevertheless, there is evidence that almost three-quarters of adults are concerned with the extent of income inequality, with 85 per cent feeling that the government should take steps to reduce it (TASC, 2009). However, with the effective disembowelling of the Combat Poverty Agency and the Equality Authority, we may not be able to mobilise factual arguments like this in the future.

Lastly, public intellectuals can show solidarity and extend the boundaries of 'me and mine'. The ethos of 'looking after your own' (family, political colleagues, class-based friends) is simultaneously Ireland's greatest strength and its Achilles heel (since it potentially legitimates corrupt practices). Kirby *et al*. (2009) argue that this very recognition of ties and obligations is a key element in the ultimate creation of social solidarity. Indeed, in a small society of less than 4.5m, it is possible to imagine a broader definition of 'our own' than that implied by family or tribe. For this to happen demands that the needs of the underprivileged and those without public voices be included in that definition of 'our own'. The threat of cutting Community Development Programmes provoked an example of cross-sector mobilisation involving academics and those in the statutory sector, as well as those in the civic and voluntary sector, in defence of programmes predominantly led and managed by women, where those being served were also part of the management structure. It may well be that this kind of initiative will become more common and it offers interesting possibilities with regard to extending the definition of 'me and mine'. In this context, the intention of the Department of Community, Rural and Gaeltacht Affairs to wind down and close the Community Development Projects in the most disadvantaged areas of the state (and the clearest example of institutional leadership provided by women) offers no reassurance about the state's ability to work with, rather than against, such forces.

Inevitably however, in the absence of violent political upheavals, the pace of change is likely to be glacial. Hence it is important to take a very long view and to focus on small achievements and particularly on consciousness raising and incremental change.

SUMMARY AND CONCLUSIONS

It seems reasonable that the kind of society most people want for themselves and their children is one that is genuinely fair: one that values children, sees women as equal partners in the home and workplace, is equally involved in the construction and transmission of knowledge and recognises the structural inequalities that still exist in our society, whether on the basis of class or gender.

Yet that very notion of fairness is being eroded. Given that our social, political and economic structures are in crisis, with confidence in both private and public power (as reflected in the market and the state) at a very low ebb, the role of public intellectuals has become increasingly important. How far such public intellectuals will be drawn from the academy remains to be seen. The extent to which they will reflect a diversity of perspectives in terms of social class and gender and will put forward visions of 'a better world' is even more problematic. If they do, they are more likely to foment informed debate and to contribute to a fundamental transformation of Irish society—eventually.

'What this crisis has done is that it has exposed the nature of power in Irish society, who has it and who hasn't it. It has also raised the question of accountability. What accountability? Accountability to whom? Who should be accountable to whom? Should people be accountable to the mass of the citizenry? These are the two issues that have been highlighted by the crisis. Whether we can do anything about them or not is another question.'

LIAM O'DOWD

'There are two words that people often put together as being essential for systems to work. One is accountability and the other is transparency. Not just the system but people need to be committed to them. I sit on a number of audit committees and there is a tendency for people to be "tick-boxish" in terms of what they do.'

FRANCES RUANE

'The problem of regulation is a problem all over the world. It may have acute poignancy here in Ireland but it has been a more general problem. It is compounded by the unwillingness of leaders to use a language of morality and ethics when they speak. What we have had instead is an increasingly technical kind of language which has emerged in a period when literally everything was privatised, not just elements of the economy but consciousness itself.'

DECLAN KIBERD

PUBLIC INTELLECTUALS AND THE 'CRISIS': ACCOUNTABILITY, DEMOCRACY AND MARKET FUNDAMENTALISM

Liam O'Dowd

School of Sociology, Social Policy and Social Work, Queen's University Belfast

INTRODUCTION

One of the ways the current economic crisis in Ireland and elsewhere has manifested itself is in a widespread crisis of public accountability—in other words, a crisis of democracy. A number of key questions have emerged including:

• What are the choices informing public policy?

• Who, or what, determines these choices?

• How, and to whom, are decision-makers and power-holders—governments, corporations, professional groupings and other institutions—to be held accountable for the consequences of the choices they make?

Such questions are scarcely new and have long preoccupied public intellectuals and critical social observers across the globe. They have now taken on a new dimension, however. The globalisation of the capitalist market and its disciplines has become the central mechanism of public

accountability. In the process, it has threatened to subor-
dinate politics and culture to its influence in many overt
and covert ways. Citizens have been recast as consumers.
Human rights are increasingly viewed through the prism
of consumption rights. Culture and identity have been
rebranded and steadily commodified. With the global and
local crises of financial capital, the contradictions inherent
in the abdication of accountability to the capitalist markets
are becoming ever more apparent.

Calls for more effective market regulation obscure the
extent to which market fundamentalism—the 'naturalisa-
tion or reification of the market' (Block, 2007, p. 327),
i.e. a vastly exaggerated belief in the ability of self-regulating markets to solve problems—has become an
unexamined tenet at the heart of advanced capitalist
society. Increased expert market regulation may promise
enhanced accountability but it does not question the relent-
less processes of commodification, or the irrationalities of
the casino capitalism practiced in global financial markets.

All capitalist crises are shaped, of course, by the particularities of time and place. The 'market' is always
embedded within particular political, social and cultural
structures. Global capitalism continues to work through,
and depend on, the international system of states and is
particularly influenced by the most powerful states in the
system, i.e. the successive hegemonies of Britain, the US
and the EU, and, more recently, by the rise of new powers
such as China, India and Brazil. The deliberations of the
G8 and G20 states reflect the changing nature of global
political economy. So, global economic crises, and the
problems they expose for democracy, manifest themselves
in variable forms in different countries. In Ireland, the
current economic crisis has served to highlight and exac-

erbate a wider crisis of public accountability that has undermined certain dominant public institutions. The very meaning of democratic accountability, of what is meant by terms like public, society and citizenship rights, has been put in question by the successive exposures of corruption and malpractice in business and the professions: the Catholic church, political parties, the Garda, the legal and medical professions and the civil service.

Potentially, at least, this has opened a space for public intellectuals to act as tribunes of democratic accountability and challenge the interlinked conventional wisdoms of market fundamentalism and technocratic expertise. Conjoined to the centrality of the 'market' is a belief in ever more specialised technocratic knowledge as the basis for political decision-making. Indeed, the idea of a 'knowledge economy', now a sort of mantra, is routinely assumed to be the high road out of the current economic crisis. Specialist expertise, however, is itself deeply commodified and structured by the 'market', and is not easily accountable to citizens in a democratic society. This has heightened the dilemma for public intellectuals. On one level, they commit themselves to raising matters of general public concern about the overall direction of society and politics (in Said's (1993) terms, they attempt to 'speak truth to power'). On another level, in contemporary societies, their request to be heard is rooted in their particular specialist or professional expertise as economists, lawyers, writers, scientists or journalists. As public intellectuals, they must decide how far they are willing to go beyond their particular competence to address broad questions of power and accountability. In doing so, they may not only undermine their status among their specialist peers, but also encourage public questioning of the nature of that expertise itself. Such questioning, however, may be one of the valuable contributions of public intellectuals to democratic societies.

Certainly, individual public intellectuals, with help from others within the state and civil society, have played important roles in exposing corruption and malpractice. Journalists such as Vincent Browne and Fintan O'Toole, for example, have consistently exposed corrupt and unaccountable practices of politicians, businessmen and other professional groups. However, this activity also exposes the fundamental structural and historical factors that limit their influence and inhibit the translation of their critiques into a sustained political challenge to the existing political and economic system: in other words, it has proved difficult to articulate real public choices or to propose sustainable forms of public accountability.

This article addresses the changing status and role of public intellectuals in Ireland and elsewhere and goes on to ask how well-equipped Irish public intellectuals are to constructively influence the current crisis. The underlying argument is that Irish intellectuals' incapacity, or unwillingness, to confront the new centrality of 'market principles' in Irish life and their impact on politics and culture greatly undermines their potential contribution to redressing the 'crisis'. Intellectual activity, including professional expertise, has become increasingly commodified in ways that have disabled analysis of the crisis of public accountability and democracy in Ireland. The prospect of a 'knowledge economy' or a 'knowledge society' has a powerful allure for intellectual workers (including public intellectuals). However, in this context, commodified knowledge is power and wealth when appropriated by corporations, professional groups and states. As such, it has the potential to further compromise the historic role of public intellectuals as social critics of power and purveyors of political choices.

THE CHANGING STATUS AND ROLE
OF PUBLIC INTELLECTUALS

Few people are willing to explicitly aspire to the status of public intellectual. To do so in Ireland has always been to court varying degrees of opprobrium—including charges of esoteric elitism and detachment from the 'real world and the concerns of real people'. The *study* of intellectuals risks additional opprobrium for adding a further layer of abstractness to an already difficult and complex subject. Nevertheless, a body of historical and social scientific analysis does exist that addresses the differential status accorded to public intellectuals cross-culturally (in France, the US and Britain, for example). Indeed, analysing the social role of intellectuals also reveals much about the societies to which they belong (Eyerman *et al.*, 1987). In a society that traditionally places a high value on conformity and cultural homogenisation, the serial critic and dissenter runs the risk of marginalisation. On the other hand, claims to 'professional status' based on having specialised knowledge meet with open or tacit social approval. Whereas the status (and, indeed, the definition) of intellectual is continually contested, that of doctors, lawyers, writers, journalists, scientists and academic specialists typically escape such criticism. Most occupational groups, such as politicians, academics, journalists, bankers, businesspeople, medics, lawyers and Garda, are keen to portray themselves as professionals, with their own specialised forms of knowledge and coteries governed by a mixture of formal and informal rules.

Of course, this tendency also has its dark side in the 'professional' criminal gangs that operate with high degrees of impunity, accountable only to their own (violent) rules, or, alternatively, among the coteries of bankers and businesspeople that operate on, or beyond, the margins of the law.

The role of the (public) intellectual remains more overtly political and contested than that of the 'professional specialist'. (In a comparative study of intellectuals, Eyerman (1996) suggests that specialists adopting the stance of public intellectual run the risk of undermining their personal and professional status among their peers. Involvement in the public arena may undermine or bolster their individual credibility or that of the professional or technical expertise on which it rests.) With the expansion of mass education, especially at third level, most public intellectuals now come from the ranks of professionalised knowledge workers who have acquired academic credentials or are employed in academia or in an occupation claiming professional status. Academia and the media provide the most important institutional framework for public intellectuals. The media claim a right and a duty to pronounce on matters of public concern while addressing a general audience or a public beyond the specialist coteries in the academy or the professions. In a small number of cases, public intellectuals may become prominent actors in political parties and government (Irish examples might include Conor Cruise O'Brien, Garrett FitzGerald and President Michael D. Higgins) but party politics is more likely to draw on 'traditional' professionals from areas such as law and teaching.

In Bauman's (1995) terms, public intellectuals challenge the 'growing fragmentation of the knowledge class caused by occupational specialisation' (p. 225). They promulgate or critique broader political or cultural projects while defining and debating the major public issues of the day (O'Dowd, 1996, pp. 3–5). The distinction between professional specialists (or intelligentsia) and intellectuals is more about the political roles that they play than about clear boundaries between two distinct groups.

In a further categorisation of intellectual activity, Bauman (1987) distinguishes between legislators and interpreters, again perhaps best understood as two types of intellectual practice:

• 'legislative': legislators are more prone to be technocratic, analytical, explanatory, prescriptive, expert, credentialist and professional. Their reference groups are their own specialist colleagues rather than wider publics; when they do address the latter they tend to see them as clients or as consumers of their specialist expertise;

• 'interpretative': interpreters are primarily concerned with 'telling stories' and with synthesis and holistic accounts. They are typically more interested in communication to diffuse audiences and prioritise access to non-specialists (via the educational system and the media) over elite prestige. They may seek to inform, mobilise or challenge wider publics rather than treat them as consumers or clients.

In practice, of course, individuals typically combine 'legislative' and 'interpretative' practice, and the 'market' may effectively commodify both.

The current economic crisis has relentlessly exposed the material basis of intellectual and broader cultural activity. It has also revealed a sense of entitlement to financial reward and self-regulation on the part of those who have wrapped themselves in the protective flag of professionalism. Demands for more public accountability on the part of doctors, clergy, civil servants, bankers, academics, politicians and businesspeople resonate with publics that are suddenly disadvantaged by the economic crisis. The resistance to such demands from the 'professional cultures' has created an opportunity for public intellectuals to challenge both complacent credentialism and the preference of the professions for self-regulation under their own formal and informal rules.

Notions of a 'society' or a 'public' to which professional specialists might be accountable have become so nebulous and fragmented, however, as to almost disappear entirely. The (knowledge) economy replaces the (knowledge) society. The result has been a kaleidoscope of sectional interests and lobbies, competing with one another for status, prestige and material resources, and occasionally investigating each other in costly, and frequently ineffectual, ways. In the Irish Republic, social partnership institutions and successive tribunals of inquiry have epitomised the fragmentation of the 'public interest' and the limits of public accountability.

To paraphrase Bauman (1987), contemporary capitalist societies are characterised by progressively fragmented and competing sites of authority—linked only by the 'market' principle—and a market-based consumerism in which ownership, control and access to resources is very unequally distributed. These sites are subsequently characterised by centralisation of ownership and control in the hands of privileged minorities. Class, gender, age, income, professional status and even ethnic background filter popular access to these minorities. In times of stability and relative economic prosperity, these elites can claim to be acting in the public, national or transnational interest. More precisely, they are able to harness unquestioned objectives of economic growth, competitiveness and consumerism to broader projects such as the building of states, nations, or forging sustainable or peaceful global order (p. 188).

Certainly, capitalist economic development has enabled vast improvements in the quality of social life in the core countries of the capitalist system. But, understood globally, it is difficult to argue that such benefits come without costs, or that they are generalisable to the mass of the world's population. More strikingly, neo-liberal capitalism has deepened social inequalities even within the richest countries, not least within Ireland. It is only when the manifest irrationalities at the heart of contemporary capitalism are exposed, and when the 'discipline' of the market is *seen* to work in highly selective, unequal and even arbitrary ways with respect to organised social groups, that the public space for critical intellectual debate expands. But how well are Irish intellectuals equipped to fill this space and address the current crisis?

HOW WELL ARE PUBLIC INTELLECTUALS EQUIPPED TO DEAL WITH THE IRISH 'CRISIS'?

For many analysts, public intellectuals are losing their influence in advanced capitalist countries (Posner, 2001). They are subsumed into a highly differentiated and specialised knowledge class that reflects the complexity of capitalist society itself. This very complexity induces a form of political paralysis, making it more difficult for public intellectuals to present clear political choices or to pronounce on the overall direction of social change. Public intellectuals may address a profusion of 'single issues' but find it difficult to formulate these in terms of contending political programmes.[1] Even if the end of ideology is not at hand, the end of the Cold War and the collapse of socialist alternatives to global capitalism have helped fracture the voice of public intellectuals. The globalisation of neo-liberal capital and related dilution of social democracy appears to have reduced the political options open, not just to political movements, but to state governments (now all subject to the discipline of global markets). Finally, in increasingly secularised societies such as Ireland, public intellectuals' proclamations of moral visions or jeremiads that dissent from the 'status quo' are met with popular scepticism.

Comparative studies of public intellectuals also indicate that national contexts matter, as do the ways in which these contexts have been formed historically (Eyerman *et al.*, 1987; O'Dowd, 1996). While the dynamics of capitalism invariably work within and through national contexts, they interact with the highly variable political and cultural formations that constitute modern states. Professionalised intellectuals do not escape the frameworks of their national states. On the contrary, their professions are symbiotically linked to the state by networks of power and material interest, even if their vocational preoccupation with rationalised and commodified knowledge transcends state boundaries. In Ireland's case, the historical formation of the national movement, its relationship with British imperialism and nationalism and the significance of the Catholic Church have all had a major influence on the status and role of the country's public intellectuals. This historical legacy continues to affect the ways in which public intellectuals address the contemporary economic crisis.

As a type, Irish nationalism is classifiable in comparative historical terms alongside nineteenth- and twentieth-century Eastern European and anti-colonial nationalisms.[2] In these movements, intellectuals played an explicit, and popularly recognised role, in 're-inventing' the national past and promulgating the vision of autonomous statehood (see Hutchinson, 1987; Garvin, 1987). They formulated a nationalist ideology that explicitly appealed to the sovereignty of a people in search of a state, rather than to the sacred nature of an existing state. Even following the emergence of the Irish state, however, public intellectuals remained preoccupied with the relationship between politics and culture, notably the uneasy fit between Irish cultural identity and the state. For many, the state failed to adequately institutionalise an Irish cultural identity that included Northern Ireland, the Irish diaspora and the many suppressed strands of the historic national movement.

On the other hand, British nationalism and its unionist manifestations on the island of Ireland relied on intellectuals' inventions to a much lesser extent. The reasons for this lie in its peculiar historical development (Nairn, 1988; Colley, 1992). Unlike most other nationalisms, its raison d'être is not supplied by intellectuals formulating visions of cultural autonomy or programmes of popular self-determination. Its myth is not of a 'sovereign people', but a celebration of the continuity and unique intrinsic merits of the British constitution. This involves making sacred key elements of the British state, such as the monarchy, parliament and army. As Colley (1992) demonstrates, the myth of an ancient English/British constitution is married to an imagined British community, originally forged in a common Protestantism (in foreign wars) in reaction to the rise of modern nationalism elsewhere, and, above all, in the imperial experience of the 'nations' of the British Isles.[3]

In Ireland, the contested nature of nation- and state-building and the lack of congruence between state and nation have insured a political prominence for public intellectuals who narrate the 'national story' or the 'national predicament'. Combined with the size of the country, this has encouraged long-standing debates over the political and cultural direction of the society as a whole. Historically, public intellectuals have been the ones to call political or clerical power-holders to account over their misappropriation or betrayal of the highest ideals of the Irish national movement or, alternatively, over the failure of that movement itself to represent the interests of Irish people. In this sense, contemporary Irish public intellectuals have a positive tradition to build on.

The particularity of Irish intellectuals and their social commentary has been shaped by three underlying but interrelated characteristics, forged in the process of state- and nation-building: personalism, institutionalism and communalism. While these characteristics also apply to public intellectuals elsewhere,[4] they form a particular constellation in Ireland that shapes the ways in which Irish intellectuals have conceived of public accountability and democracy. More significantly, this constellation in turn is influenced, in frequently unacknowledged ways, by processes of marketisation and commodification.

PERSONALISM, INSTITUTIONALISM AND COMMUNALISM

Public intellectualism in Ireland, in contrast to continental Europe, is more noted for the prominence of key personalities than for allegiance to distinct ideologies or schools of thought (Goldring, 1987).[5] While leading twentieth-century Irish intellectuals certainly had political leanings to the ideologies of right or left, they were not associated in any sustained way with camps, movements, political parties or, indeed, any institutions espousing ideological divisions.[6] This, in turn, served to marginalise debates over alternative forms of economic, political and social order—how class, patriarchy, democracy, citizenship, or civic republicanism might constitute such an order.

The dominance of the parallel institutions of church and state and the centrality of nationalism and religion marginalised much ideological debate in twentieth-century Ireland. As I have argued elsewhere, it was easier to classify Irish intellectuals in terms of their primary affiliations to state or church than to locate them as partisans of political movements and ideologies (O'Dowd, 1985). The more independent public intellectuals were mainly writers or other creative artists who had a measure of material independence from church and state in Ireland, either because they had emigrated from Ireland, or because they were able to support themselves by developing a literary and critical voice which found an audience nationally and internationally. This creative personalities tradition was exemplified by such luminaries as Joyce, Yeats, O'Casey, Synge and their literary successors.

The literary tradition, however, was to become more institutionalised and professionalised over time within the expanded university systems of Ireland and other English-speaking countries. The professionalisation of academic literary criticism, overlapping with the study of history and politics, in a new field of 'Irish Studies', has become an important framework for critically discussing the links between politics and culture in late twentieth and early twenty-first century Ireland, while largely obscuring its own material basis and that of the society it addressed.[7]

The triad of state-affiliated, church-affiliated and independent (mainly literary) public intellectuals was restructured in the last quarter of the twentieth century by the growth of the mass media as a forum and filter for Irish social commentary. The media, supported by both the state and capital (via ownership and advertising), created pundits or professional 'commentariats', who made some public intellectuals into celebrities (Regis Debray (1981) has mapped this transition in France), and turned a succession of hitherto personal troubles into public issues, mostly associated with the rights of women, married couples, children and gay people. Less obvious was the way in which the media linked the 'vanguard' social liberalism of its journalists (Corcoran, 2004) with the commodification of culture (Browne, 2004), while failing to register what Burawoy (2007) has termed the progressive marketisation of labour, money, land, and nature (including the body).[8]

Communalism, the third characteristic of Irish intellectual commentary, is deeply embedded in the history of religion, state and nation-formation in Ireland. Facilitated by partition and by the culturally homogenising agendas of Catholicism and nationalism, it prioritises the 'collectivity' over the individual. As such, it is always double-edged—it can function as a call for social solidarity or as a means of resisting domination or exploitation. Alternatively, it can incapacitate analyses of the subordination of classes, genders, new immigrants or other minorities. The 'rights' and 'wrongs' of community appeal more to the intellectual as storyteller or interpreter than to the technocratic analyst. As a form of communitarianism, communalism is

somewhat resistant to individualisation and commodification. In many of its Catholic or nationalist forms, however,
it has obscured the role of advanced capitalism in fragment-
ing social solidarity, enhancing social inequality, and
commodifying and co-opting Irish culture.[9]

FOUR CRISES

Personalism, institutionalism and communalism have been
restructured, however, by a series of four crises that have
been critical to the formation of Irish intellectuals and
their debates over the last 60 years. In line with developments elsewhere, the growth of experts and professional
specialists fragmented public debate but within an overall
binary framework. On one hand, the core political debates
in the Irish state have become progressively more economistic. On the other, Irish public intellectuals have
continued to rework the relationship between politics and
culture, while ignoring economic transformation.[10] In the
process, the structural links between politics and culture
and the changing economy remain obscured or, at least,
under-analysed.

The first crisis was the pervasive economic and social
collapse of the 1950s. The second was the challenge posed
by the crisis of Northern Ireland in the 1970s and 1980s,
the third was the fiscal and emigration crisis of the 1980s
and the fourth is the current global economic crisis and
the more general crisis of public accountability and
democracy.

The 1950s watershed is the historical transition most
frequently and repetitively celebrated by public intellectuals
in the Irish Republic. The mid-century sense of crisis was
pervasive and seemed to mark a comprehensive failure of
the Irish state to realise the objectives of the Irish national

Liam O'Dowd

project—to stem emigration, reverse population decline, achieve economic prosperity, revive the Irish language and unify the country. It also marked the end of any pretence of establishing a corporatist or redistributive social order in Ireland founded on Catholic social principles. The solution proposed by Lemass/Whitaker was a more active state promoting foreign direct investment and expanding its educational infrastructure. The new economic policy could still be presented as a way of completing the national project even if it meant downgrading other objectives such as ending partition or reviving the Irish language. The 'state' was now accorded much greater priority than the 'nation', and its policies, including joining the European Economic Community, came to be presented as the apotheosis of Irish nationalism (Hayward, 2010).

The eruption of the second crisis—the conflict in Northern Ireland—seemed an untimely challenge to the growing state-centric concerns of southern intellectuals. It resurrected unresolved questions about partition and the failures of the nationalist project. The result was an even deeper partitioning of public discourse. The North was characterised by debates over state repression, political violence and the re-emergence of nationalism, unionism, republicanism, loyalism and religion as contentious political issues. The dominant thrust of southern public debate was to externalise the conflict and present it as anachronistic, while promoting a partnership between the British and Irish governments to bring about a resolution. Revisionist historical accounts were part of this distancing and sought to convey that southern politics had become concerned with a different set of issues around economic development, state management of the economy and European integration. By the 1980s electoral politics on either side of the border existed in two almost parallel universes, one preoccupied with violent ethno-national conflict, the other with a third (economic) crisis.

The economism of intellectual discourse in the late 1970s and 1980s had also been challenged by a third crisis: a deep economic recession, which saw a huge increase in unemployment, the return of mass emigration, and a related fiscal crisis of the state. By the 1990s, however, revised state policies, US foreign investment and a global economic upturn gave birth to the Celtic Tiger phenomenon. This seemed to copper-fasten the success of economistic politics, whilst gaining added lustre from the successful 'peace process' in Northern Ireland. Suddenly the island of Ireland seemed to be the source of two effective models for export: (1) how to build a successful, small and open economy in a globalised neo-liberal economy; and (2) how to settle a durable and apparently intractable ethno-national conflict.

The fourth crisis—the global capitalist crisis from 2007 onwards—exposed the dark side of Ireland's success story: the crisis of the financial markets, the collapse of the property bubble and huge levels of public and private indebtedness revealed the consequences of embracing ever deeper forms of commodification and consumer capitalism. This manifested itself most sharply in a crisis of public accountability, which pervaded electoral politics, bureaucratic managerialism in the public service and the long-standing social partnership arrangements. The crisis had been prefigured in the various investigations and tribunals of inquiry into corruption in business, politics, public service professions and the church. Not only had accountability been compromised in each institutional sphere, the different institutions seemed incapable of

acting as checks and balances on each other.[11] The prolif-
eration of self regulation, or minimal or ineffective
regulation within the professions and among those bankers
and developers at the heart of the new capitalism, seemed
to typify the new system that had been created in Ireland's
corner of the global economy.

CONSEQUENCES FOR PUBLIC INTELLECTUALS
AND THE INTELLECTUAL FIELD

The four crises discussed above mark significant water-
sheds in the formation of Irish public intellectuals and the
wider intellectual field in which they are located. All four
facilitated a progressively economistic approach in intellectual discourse, which gradually displaced a discourse
centred on the communalism of nation and religion.
Almost imperceptibly, the central mechanism of public
accountability became the self-regulating market of new
neo-liberal consumerist capitalism.

While this market was transnational and increasingly
global, remarkably, Irish intellectual discourse became
more state-centric. At its core was a Dublin-based 'public
conversation', pursued in the print and electronic media
and represented at its apex by RTÉ and the *Irish Times*.
Kirby *et al*. (2002) have noted that this conversation was
informed by a project of creating a 'modern, liberal, progressive, multi-cultural image fashioned according to the
need for international acceptance rather than through
engagement with Ireland's past' (p. 197). In the fourth
'crisis' from 2007 onwards, nowhere has the need for
international acceptance been so pressing than in the perceived need to satisfy the 'markets'. Indeed, it appears that
the 'markets' were somehow 'external', rather than constitutive of the new Ireland that had emerged.

The state-centric focus of public intellectual discourse was combined with a persisting sense of Irish exceptionalism. The latter was not novel in the sense that it was a hallmark of much clericalist and nationalist thinking since partition. It characterised Irish public intellectuals as interpreters of Ireland's story, and pervaded the work of historians, social scientists and literary intellectuals. The 'interpreters' emphasised particularism at the expense of comparison (apart from the reflex comparisons with the UK, which gradually lost prominence with membership of the European Community). Not only was comparison downplayed, the analysis and critique of the type of global political economy and social order into which Ireland was being integrated remained a minority interest.[12] As in much anglophone mainstream intellectual and academic discourse in the late twentieth century, terms such as empire, colonialism and capitalism (Browne, 2004) were supplanted by 'modernisation', 'modernity' and 'post-modernity', for example.[13]

The project of making the Irish state sufficiently prosperous, liberal, progressive and multi-cultural certainly transformed 'private troubles' into 'public issues', generating a much enhanced critical analysis of the repressions and pieties of Irish nationalism and Catholicism.[14] The emergence of a complex feminist critique (O'Connor, 2006), the mobilisations around the individual rights of women, children, gay people, married people, migrants and other cultural minorities provided for links between the critical commentary of public intellectuals and the mobilisation of civil society organisations.

There is, however, a downside to this intellectual project. It is associated with the symbolic power of what Kirby *et al*. (2002) term a 'rhetoric of binary terror' (p.

7), where the pre-1960s history is seen as bogeyman. De Valera's Ireland is portrayed as the repository of all that is stagnant, backward looking, abusive and repressive about Irish 'tradition'. Lemass and Whitaker, perceived to be the founding fathers of post-1960s' Ireland, on the other hand, are celebrated for having ushered in an era of modernisation, progress and prosperity (see Cleary, 2007a, pp. 1–13). There is much evidence attesting to considerable material progress and to the emergence of a more open and tolerant society over the last six decades. However, the celebratory undertones consistently prevent, or inhibit, critical analysis of the contemporary social order and of Irish intellectuals' stake in it.

Exponential growth in the specialised knowledge professions and of third-level education provided vastly expanded opportunities for intellectuals in Ireland and abroad. The institutionalist basis of Irish intellectuals was no longer the narrowly defined establishments of church and state; rather, it took the form of an inter-connected network of professional organisations now implicated in an unprecedented commodification of knowledge and culture registering the demands of state and market. In the process, a fundamentalist belief in the self-regulating market as the ultimate mechanism of public accountability took hold. The ideological compartmentalisation of economy from politics and culture, long a characteristic of Irish intellectual commentary, acquired new forms.

While intellectuals proclaimed the merits of economic globalisation, Irish communalism was reshaped as speaking to, and on behalf of, the Irish state. The implications of the marketisation of the Irish state itself, while glimpsed in particular debates over privatisation, were obscured with the shift from government to governance. With some exceptions, cultural intellectuals rather underplayed the negative consequences of marketisation. As Michael Burawoy (2007) observes, the state in capitalist society was no longer a bulwark or even a major constraint on this process—rather it was itself transformed by the process, something that was largely unremarked upon by Irish intellectuals. In important ways, the state was being fragmented and partially denationalised by its participation in the global economy. Privatisation, Europeanisation and foreign direct investment were pushing the Irish state into a much altered role: coordinating and managing forces that lay well outside its control. Like other capitalist states, it was to be a conductor of economic growth, consumerism and commodification rather than a means of realising social and cultural goals. This new role created major new opportunities for legislators, technocrats and experts organised on a professional basis, not just in Ireland but in transnational, professional and governance organisations in Anglo-America and Europe.

As the state increasingly becomes the servant and collaborator of individual and corporate capitalists, its public service functions are privatised, for example the privatisation of specialist advice as private consultancy firms become ever more important as advisors to government. With the commercial ownership of this form of knowledge, public accountability is further reduced, as the bases on which government decisions are taken become less publically accessible.

For many Irish intellectuals, the market fundamentalism of the Celtic Tiger period seemed to offer a (somewhat unacknowledged) escape from the repressiveness of nationalism, religion and the dogmatism of rightist and leftist ideologies. In the process, however, market ideology acted as a blind on the self-knowledge of Irish intellectuals. Nowhere is this more evident than in the far-reaching commodification of Irish culture.

'Culture', in its various creative and artistic forms, has long been a standpoint from which to critique politics. It has gradually become an object for commodification (Peillon, 2002), i.e. selling Ireland, while rebranding its cultural distinctiveness, has become yet another means of boosting economic growth and consumerism. Music, dance, literature and the visual arts are now export commodities in the globalised Ireland of the Celtic Tiger. The literary giants of the Irish cultural revival, and some of their successors, themselves became objects of tourist promotion—of entertainment rather than criticism. The personalism of the Irish intellectual tradition has survived, albeit often in the form of individual media celebrity. One of the historic hallmarks of Irish intellectual commentary, its tendency to focus on the exceptionalism or particularities of the Irish experience, has now become a prime market resource. Indeed, the case for capitalising the distinctiveness of Irish culture has been argued at length by Bradley and Kennelly (2008) (for critique, see Inglis, 2009).

The 'market' has replaced repression with seduction, however. The recent economic crisis has exposed the irrationalities and contradictions at the heart of global capitalism and revealed the extent to which Irish intellectuals have become beneficiaries of the new order. Intellectuals were not merely 'bought off' in a crude manner; indeed, many highlighted the inequities and contradictions of the new order. However, the inherited traditions of personalism, institutionalism and communalism have rendered them ill-prepared to respond to the crisis and address the extent to which the mantle of public accountability has shifted from 'politics' to the 'market'. The deep-rooted tendency to compartmentalise economic debates from those regarding the relationship between politics and culture reflected a persistent philosophical idealism. Economic debates are ever more technocratic, the preserve of 'legislators' in Bauman's (1987) sense. Debates on politics and culture meanwhile remain the preserve of the 'interpreters' and fail to register the extent to which both are co-opted by the market.

The traditional institutions which once facilitated the activity of public intellectuals in Ireland have also been heavily compromised. The Catholic Church, undergoing a fundamental institutional crisis of its own, had never in any case supported a convincing alternative to the economic status quo. The Irish state has become more fragmented and marketised. Perhaps more significantly for public intellectuals, their central platform—the nexus between the media and academia—has itself become deeply compromised by 'market values' (Browne, 2004). The universities are increasingly marketised, bureaucratically managed and encouraged to act as economic development corporations and prove their economic utility. Meanwhile, the media, heavily dependent on commercial advertising, is scarcely receptive to critiques of market fundamentalism.

While the marketisation of institutions inhibits critical intellectual commentary, it does not preclude it. The current crisis, in exposing the precariousness of the global economic order and the irrationalities and inequities that inform it, provides new opportunities for critical public intellectuals. Moreover, some of the historical legacies of Irish state and nation-building are enabling rather than disabling in forging a more constructive role for public intellectuals in the current crisis.

Liam O'Dowd

Conclusions

One of the positive outcomes of the contemporary economic crisis is a certain intensification of debate about the role of public intellectuals and professional experts. Examples include the media debates across a range of platforms among academic and corporate economists over the banking crisis and government economic policy, and ongoing debates in the *Irish Times* over the role of universities and academics (see for example Hess, 2009; Garvin, 2010 and this volume; Sterling, 2010).

This debate is impaired, however, by a failure to acknowledge the extent to which 'market fundamentalism' has replaced nationalism, religion and traditional political ideologies of right and left. This failure is linked to a long-standing tendency to compartmentalise and reify the 'economy' as an unquestioned 'fact of nature'. For example, the fetish for property and a taboo on property taxes (replacing the old taboo on sex?) are often among the unspoken assumptions of (acceptable) public discourse. In these circumstances, the new centrality of the 'market' has compromised democracy and public accountability in Ireland as it has in many other countries. The transformation of citizens into mere consumers (or into producers of market commodities) has deeply reshaped the roles, expectations and practices of public intellectuals and of professional specialists in the academy, state agencies and the corporate economy. 'Speaking truth to power' takes on a different meaning when knowledge is power and intellectuals and professional specialists are significant power-holders themselves. This puts a premium on self-knowledge and reflexivity and on questioning to whom, or to what, are intellectuals and professional specialists accountable? Mantras such as the 'knowledge economy', or 'knowledge for knowledge's sake', if not critically examined, do little for public account-ability or democracy generally.

Is the primary 'duty' of experts and professional experts to produce commodified knowledge for the market on the unexamined assumptions that economic growth, however defined, is a public good? Do academics or third-level students, financed by tax-payers, have any responsibility for public service beyond maximising their incomes and meeting market demand? Is accountability to professional peers or to self-regulating professional bodies sufficient in an era when the negative consequences of defective public regulation are all too apparent?

To pose the issue as merely one of regulatory failure, however, is surely to beg many questions that public intel-lectuals themselves might raise. For example, who will regulate, in what manner, and in whose interests? Contemporary public intellectuals are typically trained in some specialist form of expertise, therefore they are well placed to ask how such specialist knowledge can be mobilised for the public good and how the 'public good' is to be defined and communicated. The way in which public intellectuals and experts engage in dialogue with civil society, with groups that challenge the state and market, and the equation of state, economy and society, is critical. These groups are not merely clients or con-sumers to be informed and satisfied. Public intellectuals can highlight the important forms of social knowledge that exist beyond the realms of universities, corporations or government departments. These forms may point to the limits of commodification, and to the need to continually question binary distinctions between experts and non-experts, between elite and popular knowledge, and between high and low culture.

I have outlined some of the factors that have enabled and disabled the role of public intellectuals in Ireland. Contemporary Irish intellectuals inherit a tradition of debate on the parallels between politics and culture, intimately linked to the history of nation- and state-building. This gives them a recognised status and role that is lacking where powerful states have predated the 'nation.' They have excelled as interpreters and story tellers; however, their focus on politics and culture has too heavily emphasised Irish exceptionalism and particularity. Ironically, it is the latter that has been deeply commodified in the contemporary global market-place. In turn, this exposes the historic compartmentalisation of 'economics' from politics/culture in Irish intellectual commentary. The progressive economisation of public debates, along with the failure to recognise the full extent of how consumer capitalism has penetrated and co-opted the state, politics and culture, marginalises the capacity of public intellectuals to enhance public accountability and democracy. This capacity is further undermined by often unacknowledged adherence to market fundamentalism—to the idea that the market is the ultimate arbiter of accountability. The markets are not 'external' to Irish society, they help constitute it. The role of public intellectuals in the current crisis is surely to problematise the way in which the various forms of market capitalism shape public choice and accountability and work through Irish politics, culture and society.

NOTES

The Assault on Intellectualism in Irish Higher Education

[1] For a comparative perspective, see similar developments in the United States: Jacoby (2008).

Public Intellectuals in Times of Crisis: The Role of Academia

[1] Posner, writing in a pre-blog world, noted the striking contrast of regulation of ideas as between the world of academia and of public intellectuals. Where the public intellectual pronounces rather than questions, he/she is at greater risk of being wrong but this risk is not great due to the lack of what Posner describes as 'quality control' in this market.

[2] In effect, they know fully the answer to the question they pose to the academic before they ask it, so the academic's purpose is to add credence to the knowledge imparted.

[3] For examples, see Cooper (2009); Ross (2009); O'Toole (2009); Leahy (2009); McWilliams (2009); Murphy (2009); Coleman (2009); Sweeney (2009); and Power (2009).

[4] Following the onset of the crisis there were numerous seminars on the issues which were well attended by academic economists, journalists, policy-makers and private sector economists.

Public Intellectuals and the 'Crisis': Accountability, Democracy and Market Fundamentalism

[1] They share this difficulty with political parties in democratic societies now rendered less cohesive by overarching social ideologies.

[2] There was a strong strand of imperial Irish nationalism that took constitutional forms, which effectively ended with partition (Anderson & O'Dowd, 2007). Thereafter this nationalism, along with majority ele-

ments in Sinn Féin, gradually transmuted into a 26-county state nationalism.

[3] The bearer of the historic mantle of the British imperial state is now the US state with its exceptionalist ideology based on the intrinsic merits of its constitution and its proclaimed civilising mission to bring freedom, democracy, the rule of law and 'free markets' to the rest of the world. Unlike its British antecedent, American ideology has found deep support in Irish intellectual life rooted in the complex historical links between Ireland and the formation of the US and a contemporary material base in the key role of US corporations in the Irish economy.

[4] No understanding of public intellectuals, of course, can ignore the influence of famous personalities. In the twentieth century, intellectuals such as Sartre, de Beauvoir, Fanon, Arendt, Sakharov, Said and Chomsky have helped to define and exemplify the role of the public intellectual in transcending their own specialist competences to address issues of public and transnational concern.

[5] Maurice Goldring (1987) characterised this phenomenon as 'personalised' intellectualism in a country 'where history is autobiographical and autobiography is historical' (pp. 9–10).

[6] The social commentary produced here has been largely, if not exclusively, idealist, in a philosophical sense; it has been preoccupied with questions of Irish identity, neglecting the material dimension (O'Dowd, 1987).

[7] Cleary (2007a) is one of the few in the field of critical literary studies who addresses the links between capital and culture as well as those between politics and culture. Adopting a historical materialist approach, he also notes how partly adversarial, partly overlapping ideologies, such as revisionism, feminism and post-colonialism, constitute the field of Irish studies. Meagher's (2001) anthropology of Irish intellectuals also categorises them under these three ideological headings but within an overall framework of how they contest modern notions of Irishness.

[8] The printed and electronic media are replete with (and dependent on) the promotion of consumerism: 'my body, my improved mind, my house, my clothes, my lifestyle, my personalized therapies, even my green environment'. (For a strong critique see Kirby, *et al.* (2002)).

[9] Communalism has been mobilised by social conservatives to oppose liberal agitation for individual rights, but it sometimes helps to mobilise

solidarity against the 'creative destruction' of consumer capitalism. See for example, Kirby et al. (2002) and Ging et al. (2009), who appeal to the communalism of 'civil society' (outside the state and the market) as a bulwark against the depredations of consumer capitalism.

[10] There are outstanding exceptions to this generalisation: see, for example, Cleary (2007a) and Kirby et al. (2002).

[11] The overarching rule of law and the legal profession was compromised by the persistent capacity of 'white collar' criminals to evade justice, and by the huge expense to tax-payers of long drawn out and often inconclusive tribunals of inquiry. This involved a transfer of public resources to an elite in the legal profession employed in the tribunals.

[12] There are notable exceptions, of course, to this generalisation: see Kirby et al., (2002, p. 4) for a summary of critiques of orthodox economic analyses. See also Crotty, 1996 and Mjoset 1992 and the post-colonial strand in Irish history and literary criticism (Carroll & King, 2003). The comparative framework of post-colonial studies is an important element in 'Irish studies' and reflects Irish academics' integration into North American, British and, to a lesser extent, European universities.

[13] The current crisis has highlighted a renewal of interest in imperialism, colonialism and capitalism, which at least hint at the importance of a critical, comparative and historical understanding of changing power relationships (Cleary, 2007a; Anderson & O'Dowd, 2007).

[14] For a perceptive and critical analysis of this project developed by Ireland's 'gateway pundits', Conor Cruise O'Brien and Fintan O'Toole, see O'Séaghdha (2002). For a somewhat different critique of 'Celtic Tiger' ideology, see Coulter and Coleman (2003).

BIBLIOGRAPHY

Anderson, J., & O'Dowd, L. (2007). Imperialism and nationalism: The Home Rule struggle and border creation in Ireland, 1885–1925. *Political Geography, 26*(8), 934–951.

Baker, J., Lynch, K., Cantillon, S., & Walsh, J. (2004, 2nd edn 2009). *Equality: From theory to action*. Hampshire: Palgrave Macmillan.

Bauman, Z. (1987). *Legislators and interpreters*. Cambridge: Polity Press.

Bauman, Z. (1995). *Life in fragments: Essays in postmodern morality*. Oxford: Blackwell.

Billig, M. (1995). *Banal nationalism*. London: Sage.

Block, F. (2007). Confronting market fundamentalism: Doing public economic sociology. *Socio-Economic Review, 5*(2), 327–333.

Bourdieu, P. (1991). Fourth lecture: The role of intellectuals in the modern world. *Poetics Today, 12*(4), National Literatures/Social Spaces, 655–669.

Bradley, F., & Kennelly, J.J. (2008). *Capitalising on culture, competing on difference, innovation, learning and a sense of place in a globalising Ireland*. Dublin: Blackhall.

Browne, H. (2004). Consenting to capital in the Irish media. *Irish Journal of Sociology, 18*(2), 129–141.

Burawoy, M. (2005). 2004 American Sociological Association Presidential Address: For public sociology. *The British Journal of Sociology, 56*(2), 258–294 (reprinted from *American Sociological Review, 70*(1), and presented at Workshop on Public Sociology at the National University of Ireland, Maynooth, March 2005).

Burawoy, M. (2007). Public sociology vs. the market. *Socio-Economic Review, 5*(2), 356–367.

Burawoy, M. Redefining the public university: Developing an analytical framework. Available at: www.public-sphere.ssrc.org/burawoy-redefining-the-public-unive rsity (accessed 2 September 2011).

Carroll, C., & King, P. (Eds.). (2003). *Ireland and postcolonial theory*. South Bend: University of Notre Dame Press.

Clancy, P. (2001). College entry in focus: A fourth national survey of access to higher education. Dublin: Higher Education Authority.

Cleary, J. (2007a). *Outrageous fortune: Capital and culture in modern Ireland*. Dublin: Field Day Publications.

Cleary, J. (2007b). Amongst empire: A short history of Ireland and empire studies in international context. *Éire-Ireland, 42*(1–2), 11–57.

Coleman, M. (2009). *Back from the brink*. Dublin: Transworld Ireland.

Colley, L. (1992). *Britons: Forging the nation, 1707–1837*. New Haven: Yale University Press.

Cooper, M. (2009). *Who really runs Ireland?* Dublin: Penguin.

Connell, R.W. (1987). *Gender and power*. Cambridge: Polity Press.

Connell, R.W. (1995). *Masculinities* (2nd edn). Cambridge: Polity Press.

Connell, R.W. (2002). *Gender*. Cambridge: Polity Press.

Corcoran, M. (2004). The political preferences and value orientations of Irish journalists. *Irish Journal of Sociology, 18*(2), 23–42.

Coulter, C., & Coleman, S. (Eds.). (2003). *The end of Irish history: Critical reflections on the Celtic Tiger*. Manchester: Manchester University Press.

Cronin, M., Kirby, P., & Ging, D. (2009). Transforming Ireland: Challenges. In M. Cronin, P. Kirby, & D. Ging

(Eds.), *Transforming Ireland: Challenges, critiques, resources* (pp. 1–20). Manchester: Manchester University Press.

Crotty, R. (1986). *Ireland in crisis: A study in capitalist colonial underdevelopment*. Tralee: Brandon Press.

Cruise O'Brien, C. (1972). *States of Ireland*. London: Panther.

Debray, R. (1981). *Teachers, writers and celebrities: The intellectuals of modern France*. London: Verson.

Economic and Social Research Institute. (2008). *Quarterly Economic Commentary*. Dublin: Economic and Social Research Institute.

Eyerman, R. (1996). Intellectuals in historical and comparative context. In L. O'Dowd (Ed.), *On intellectuals and intellectual life in Ireland* (pp. 31–51). Belfast: Queen's University & Dublin: Royal Irish Academy.

Eyerman, R., Sevensson, L.G., & Soderqvist, T. (Eds.). (1987). *Intellectuals, universities and the state in Western modern societies*. Berkeley: University of California Press.

Fahey, T. (1990). Measuring the female labour force supply: Conceptual and procedural problems in Irish official statistics. *Economic and Social Review, 2*(2), 163–191.

FitzGerald, J., Bergin, A., Barrett, A., Duffy, D., Garrett, S., & McCarthy, Y. (2005). *Mid-term review: 2005–2012*. Dublin: Economic and Social Research Institute.

Garvin, T. (1987). *Nationalist revolutionaries in Ireland, 1858–1928*. Oxford: Clarendon Press.

Garvin, T. (2010, May 1). Grey philistines taking over our universities. *Irish Times*, p. 15.

Ging, D. (2009). All consuming images: New gender formations in post-Celtic Tiger Ireland. In M. Cronin, P. Kirby, & D. Ging (Eds.), *Transforming Ireland: Challenges, critiques, resources* (pp. 52–72). Manchester: Manchester University Press.

Goldring, M. (1987). *Faith of our fathers: A study of Irish nationalism*. Dublin: Repsol Publishing.

Gramsci, A. (1971). *Selections from the prison notebooks*. Q. Hoare, & G. Nowell Smith (Eds. & trans.). London: Lawrence and Wishart.

Grummell, B., Lynch, K., & Devine, D. (2009). Appointing senior managers in education: Homosociability, local logics and authenticity in the selection process. *Educational Management, Administration and Leadership, 37*(3), 329–349.

Hayward, K. (2010). European stories as national narratives: Irish intellectuals on 'Europe'. In J. Lacroix & K. Nicolaidis (Eds.), *European stories: Intellectual debates on Europe in National Contexts* (pp. 167–182). Oxford: Oxford University Press.

Hess, A. (2009, October 31). Time to consider our position as citizens and not consumers. *Irish Times*, p. 13.

Hess, A. (2009, February 16). Third-level revolution sees conformity replace creativity. *Irish Times*.

Higgins, M. D. (2012). 'The role of the university at a time of intellectual crisis'. Address by President Michael D. Higgins on receipt of Doctorate of Laws from the National University of Ireland. Dublin Castle, 25 January.

Humphreys, P., Drew, E., & Murphy, C. (1999). *Gender equality in the Irish civil service*. Dublin: Institute of Public Administration.

Husu, L. (2006). Gate-keeping, gender and recognition of scientific excellence. Paper presented at XVI ISA World Congress of Sociology, Durban.

Hutchinson, J. (1987). *The dynamics of cultural nationalism: The Gaelic revival and the creation of the Irish nation state*. London: Allen and Unwin.

Bibliography

Inglis, T. (2009). Getting and spending. *Dublin Review of Books, 9*, www.drb.ie/archive.aspx (accessed 11 November 2011).

Jacoby, S. (2008). *The age of American unreason*. London: Random House.

Joffe, J. (2003). The decline of the public intellectual and the rise of the pundit. In A.M. Melzer, J. Weinberger, & M.R. Zinman (Eds.), *The public intellectual: Between philosophy and politics* (pp. 109–22). Oxford: Rowman & Littlefield Publishers, Inc.

Jordan, D., & O'Leary, E. (2007). Is Irish innovation policy working? Evidence from Irish technology businesses. *Journal of the Statistical and Social Inquiry Society of Ireland, (37)*, 1–43.

Judt, T. (2010). *Ill fares the land*. New York. Penguin.

Kirby, P., Gibbons, L., & Cronin, M. (Eds.). (2002). *Reinventing Ireland: Culture, society and the global economy*, London: Pluto Press.

Kane, E. (1996). The power of paradigms: Social science and intellectual contributions to public discourse in Ireland. In L. O'Dowd (Ed.), *On intellectuals and intellectual life in Ireland*. Belfast: Queens University; Dublin: Royal Irish Academy.

Kelly, J. (2009, 16 April). New master plan needed for higher education. *Irish Times*.

Kelly, M. (2007). On the likely extent of falls in Irish house prices. In Economic and Social Research Institute, *Quarterly Economic Commentary* (pp. 45–54).

Kronman, A. T. (2007). *Education's end: Why our colleges and universities have given up on the meaning of life*. New Haven: Yale University Press.

Leahy, P. (2009). *Showtime*. Dublin: Penguin.

Leonard, M. (2004). Teenage girls and housework in Irish society. *Irish Journal of Sociology, 13*(1), 73–85.

Lightman, A. (2000). The role of the public intellectual. MIT Communications Forum, http://web.mit.edu/comm-forum/papers/lightman.html (accessed 17 February 2012).

Lukes, S. (1974). *Power: A radical view.* London: Macmillan.

Lynch, K. (1989). Solidary labour: Its nature and marginalisation. *Sociological Review, 37*(1), 1–14.

Lynch, K. (1994). Women teach and men manage: Why men dominate senior posts in Irish education. In *Women for leadership in education.* Dublin: Education Commission of the Conference of Religious in Ireland.

Lynch, K. (1999a). Equality studies, the academy and the role of research in emancipatory social change. *Economic and social review, 30*, 41–69.

Lynch, K (1999b). *Equality in education.* Dublin: Gill and Macmillan.

Lynch, K., Crean, M., & Moran, M. (2009). Equality and social justice: The university as a site of struggle. Unpublished manuscript.

Lynch, K., & Lodge, A. (2002). *Equality and power in schools: Redistribution, recognition and representation.* London: Routledge.

Lynch, K., & Lyons, M. (2008). The gendered order of caring. In U. Barry (Ed.), *Where are we now? New feminist perspectives on women in contemporary Ireland.* New Island: Think Tank for Action on Social Change (Ireland) (TASC).

McCoy, S., & Smyth, E. (2004). *At work in school.* Dublin: Liffey Press, in association with the Economic and Social Research Institute.

McDonough, T., & Loughrey, J. (2009). *The HEAP chart: Hierarchy of earnings, attributes, and privilege analysis.* Dublin: TASC.

McGinnity, F. and Russell, H. (2008). Gender Inequalities in Time Use. Dublin: ESRI and Equality Authority, http://www.equality.ie/index.asp?locID=105&docID=725 (accessed 25 September 2011).

McLaughlin, N. (2011). Public Intellectuals and Public Academics: Rhetoric and Realities. Paper presented at Department of Sociology, University College Dublin, 29 September 2011.

McWilliams, D. (2009). *Follow the money*. Dublin: Gill & Macmillan.

Meagher, D. M. (2001). *Academic rites: An anthropology of contested reproductions of modern Irishness*. Unpublished PhD thesis, National University of Ireland Maynooth.

Miliband, R. (1982). *Capitalist democracy in Britain*. Oxford: Oxford University Press.

Mjoset, L. (1992). *The Irish economy in a comparative institutional perspective*. Dublin: National Economic and Social Council.

Murphy, D. (2009). *Banksters*. Dublin: Hachette.

N.A. (1957, September). 'Get to work! They're saying I have no future!' *Dublin Opinion*.

Nairn, T. (1988). *The enchanted glass: Britain and its monarchy*. London: Radius.

NYCI (2010). http://www.nwci.ie/ (accessed 30 October 2009).

O'Connor, F. (1962, February 15). Censorship system criticised. *Irish Independent*, p. 3.

O'Connor, P. (1996). Organisational culture as a barrier to women's promotion. *Economic and Social Review, 27*(3), 187–216.

O'Connor, P. (2003). Feminism and the politics of gender. In M. Ashead, & M. Millar (Eds.), *Public administration and public policy* (pp. 54–68). London: Routledge.

O'Connor, P. (2006). Private troubles, public issues: The Irish sociological imagination. *Irish Journal of Sociology, 15*(2), 5–22.

O'Connor, P. (2008a). *Irish children and teenagers in a changing world*. Manchester: Manchester University Press.

O'Connor, P. (2008b). The elephant in the corner: Gender and policies related to higher education. *Administration, 56*(1), 85–110.

O'Connor, P. (2008c). The Irish patriarchal state: Continuity and change. In M. Adshead, P. Kirby, & M. Millar (Eds.), *Contesting the state: Lessons from the Irish case* (pp. 143–164). Manchester: Manchester University Press.

O'Connor, P. (2010). Gender and organisational culture at senior management level: Limits and possibilities for change? In J. Harford & C. Rush (Eds.), *Have women made a difference? Women in Irish universities, 1850–2010* (pp. 139–162). Oxford: Peter Lang.

O'Connor, P. (2010). Is senior management in Irish universities male dominated? What are the implications? *Irish Journal of Sociology, 18*(1), 1–21.

O'Dowd, L. (1985). Intellectuals and social ideology in twentieth-century Ireland and the case of George Russell (AE). *Crane Bag, 9*, 6–25.

O'Dowd, L. (1988). Neglecting the material dimension: Irish intellectuals and the problem of identity. *Irish Review, 3*, 8–17.

O'Dowd, L. (1991). Intellectuals and political culture: A unionist-nationalist comparison. In E. Hughes (Ed.), *Culture and politics in Northern Ireland, 1960–1990* (pp. 151–173). Milton Keynes: Open University Press.

O'Dowd, L. (1996). Intellectuals and intelligentsia: A sociological introduction. In L. O'Dowd (Ed.), *On intellectuals and intellectual life in Ireland: International, comparative and historical contexts* (pp. 1–30). Belfast: Institute of Irish Studies, & Dublin: Royal Irish Academy.

O'Dowd, S. (2009). Position Paper on Community Development Programme. Unpublished manuscript, Ballyphehane-Togher, CDP, Cork.

O'Hagan, C. (2010). Inequalities and Privileges: Middle-class mothers and employment. Unpublished PhD thesis, University of Limerick.

Ó Seaghdha, B. (2002). The Celtic Tiger's media pundits. In P. Kirby, L. Gibbons, & M. Cronin (Eds.). *Reinventing Ireland: Culture, society and the global economy* (pp. 143–159). London: Pluto Press.

O'Toole, F. (2009). *Ship of fools*. Dublin: Faber & Faber.

Peillon, M, (2002). 'Culture and state in Ireland's new economy'. In P. Kirby *et al*. (Eds.). *Reinventing Ireland: Culture, society and the global economy*. London: Pluto Press (pp. 38–53).

Posner, R.A. (2001). *Public intellectuals: A study of decline*. Cambridge MA: Harvard University Press.

Power, J. (2009). *Picking up the pieces*. Dublin: Blackhall Publishing.

Purves, L. (2009, 14 December). List mania is the besetting folly of our age. *The Times*.

Ransome, P. (1992). *Antonio Gramsci: A new introduction*. Hertfordshire: Harvester Wheatsheaf.

Ross, S. (2009). *The bankers*. Dublin: Penguin.

Rottman, D. (1994). *Income distribution within Irish households*. Dublin: Combat Poverty.

Russell. H., McGinnity, F., Callan, T., & Keane, C. (2009). *A woman's place: Female participation in the Irish labour market*. Dublin: ESRI and the Equality Authority.

Russell, H., Smyth, E., & O'Connell, P. (2005). *Degrees of equality: Gender pay differentials among recent graduates*. Dublin: Economic and Social Research Institute.

Said, E. (1993). Speaking truth to power (Reith Lectures, reprinted in the *Independent*, 24 June, 1, 8, 15, 22, and 29 July).

Sartre, J.P. (1974). *Between existentialism and Marxism*. London: Verso.

Sheehan, J. (2005). Review of national policies for education: Review of higher education in Ireland: Examiner's report. *Economic and Social Review, 36*(1), 67–75.

Simcox, R. (2009). *A degree of influence*. London: Centre for Social Cohesion.

Sterling, S. (2010, June 3). Public conversation on universities is welcome, *Irish Times*, p. 13.

Sullivan, D. (2009). *Cultural politics and Irish education since the 1950s: Policy, paradigms and power*. Dublin: Institute of Public Administation.

Sweeney, A. (2009). *Banana republic*. Dublin: Gill & Macmillan.

TASC. (2009). *The solidarity factor: Public responses to economic inequality in Ireland*. Dublin: Think Tank for Action on Social Change (Ireland).

Turner, T., & D'Art, D. (2005). *Is there a knowledge economy in Ireland?* Limerick: PER, Working Paper Research Series, Number 07/05.

Whitaker, T.K. (1958). *Economic development*. Dublin: Stationery Office.

Wright Mills, C. (1956) (2nd edn 1970). *The power elite*. New York. Oxford University Press.

Wright Mills, C. (1970). *The sociological imagination*. Middlesex: Pelican.

ABOUT THE CONTRIBUTORS

Donncha O'Connell

Donncha O'Connell is a qualified barrister and lecturer in law at the National University of Ireland, Galway, where he teaches constitutional law, European human rights, processes of law reform and advocacy, activism and public interest law. He is also a part-time commissioner of the Law Reform Commission. He was appointed to the Legal Aid Board in 2011 and has been a member of the board of INTERIGHTS since 2009. He is the founder and editor of the *Irish Human Rights Law Review*. Donncha was dean of Law at NUI Galway from 2005–08 after which he was a Visiting Senior Fellow at the Centre for the Study of Human Rights, London School of Economics. Since 2006 he has been a director of the internationally acclaimed Druid Theatre Company. He is a regular contributor to English and Irish language print and broadcast media on legal and political affairs.

Tom Garvin

Professor Tom Garvin has lectured in politics at University College Dublin since 1967, where he is now emeritus professor. He is the author of many books and articles on Irish and comparative politics. These include *The evolution of Irish nationalist politics* (1981), *Nationalist revolutionaries in Ireland* (1987), *Preventing the future* (2004), *1922: the birth of Irish democracy* (1996), *Judging Lemass* (2009) and *News from a new republic* (2011). He holds a PhD from the University of Georgia and is an alumnus of the Woodrow Wilson International Center for Scholars, Washington DC. He has twice been a William Fulbright scholar and has been visiting professor at five American universities. He was a founding member of the Irish Political Studies Association. He has taught Irish politics, US constitutional history, politics of nationalism, communism, international relations, comparative politics and research methods.

Frances Ruane

Professor Frances Ruane is director of the Economic and Social Research Institute. She previously lectured at the Department of Economics in Trinity College Dublin, where she was also director of the Policy Institute and of the MSc in Economic Policy Studies. A graduate of University College Dublin and the University of Oxford, she is an Honorary Fellow of Trinity College Dublin and a member of the Royal Irish Academy, the Council of the Statistical and Social Inquiry Society of Ireland and the editorial boards of the Journal of International and Economic Policy and the International Review of Economics and Finance. She is currently a member of the Health Research Board, the National Pensions Reserve Fund Commission, the Economic Advisory Group in Northern Ireland and the Council of Economic Advisors in Scotland. She has published extensively in the fields of international economic and industrial development. Her current research explores enterprises, productivity and trade.

Pat O'Connor

Pat O'Connor is professor of sociology and social policy at the University of Limerick, where she was executive (and founding) dean of the Faculty of Arts, Humanities and Social Sciences (2000–10). She has worked at Bedford and Royal Holloway College, University of London; the National Institute of Social Work; the Waterford Institute of Technology and the Economic and Social Research Institute and has been visiting professor at four universities around the world. Her area of expertise is the structural and cultural reality of gender, and the ways in which gender is simultaneously ignored and maintained in a variety of contexts including the state, higher education and the family. She is interested in the role that public sociology can play in this context. Her books include *Friendships between women* (1992), *Emerging voices: women in contemporary Irish society* (1998) and *Irish children and teenagers in a changing world* (2008). She chaired the International Panel for the allocation of Linnaeus funding and is a reviewer for the European Science Foundation.

Liam O'Dowd

Liam O'Dowd is professor of sociology at Queen's University Belfast and director of the Centre for International Borders Research. A founder member of the Sociological Association of Ireland, he served as chairman of the Royal Irish Academy National Committee for Economics and Social Sciences (1992–96). His research interests encompass the study of state borders, the political economy of the Northern Ireland conflict, urban sociology, the political sociology of intellectuals and the ideologies of imperialism, republicanism, British and Irish nationalism. Since 2007, in conjunction with colleagues in the Universities of Cambridge and Exeter, he has led a Queen's research team in an interdisciplinary ESRC-funded research project entitled 'Conflict in cities and the contested state: everyday life and possibilities of transformation in Belfast, Jerusalem and other divided cities' (www.conflictincities.org).